Roots and Wings

For friends in Peace
Rose Lucey

Resource Publications, Inc.
160 E. Virginia St. No. 290
San Jose, CA 95112

Editorial Director: Kenneth Guentert
Cover Design and Production Artist: Ron Niewald
ISBN 0-89390-113-X
Printed and Bound in the United States of America 5 4 3 2 1

Copyright © 1987 by Resource Publication, Inc. All Rights Reserved. For reprint permission, write Reprint Department, Resource Publications, Inc., 160 E. Virginia St. No. 290, San Jose, CA 95112.

TABLE of CONTENTS

Foreword by Henri Nouwen	vi
Prologue	ix
An Opening Word	xi
Chapter I: *Gifts*	1
Chapter II: *To Tell a Story*	9
Chapter III: *To Educate and Activate*	15
Chapter IV: *Companions on the Way*	29
Chapter V: *Stretching the Boundaries*	41
Chapter VI: *The Turbulent Years*	61
Chapter VII *The Genius of CFM*	83
Chapter VIII *A New Moment*	101
Programs of the CFM *1951-1987*	129
Index	131

ACKNOWLEDGEMENTS

I write this book in a spirit of gratitude and as a loving tribute to the long line of families, sisters and clergy who, for forty years, grappled with the challenge to make the Gospel alive in their own homes and in the marketplace.

Thanks are due to Canon Joseph Cardijn, people priest of Belgium, who brought to birth the concept of Observe-Judge-Act. To priest-prophet Louis Putz, of the Holy Cross Order.

There is no way to name all the men and women whose lives were changed by the challenge to take the Gospel into their everyday lives and act for justice. To the pioneers, I am grateful: Pat and Patty Crowley, Bishop Charles Buswell, priests Peter Sammon, the brothers Eschweiler, Bill and Lena Mimiaga, Louis Putz of the Holy Cross order, Helene and Bernie Bauer, and so many others who were tireless in fostering the movement across the nation.

When I appealed for stories of how CFM had affected personal lives, letters came from young people, women and men who said, "Life can never be the same." I take this opportunity to thank them for sharing beautiful stories of struggle and success, a hidden history of the families of the American Catholic experience.

It was around a dining room table at the home of Reggie and Ralph Weissert in South Bend, Indiana, that Patty Crowley, Dennis Geaney, Madelyn and Joe Bonsignore, and Dan and I sat, talking about writing a history of the Christian Family Movement. We knew the impact of CFM on our lives and the Church and agreed the story had to be told. I owe a special thanks to them for the origin of the dream I was impelled to pursue.

I am indebted to the many people who shared their stories of life in CFM, and to Kay and Gary Aitchison of the National Office for giving me unstinting assistance and free reign to use all CFM materials.

Encouragement came from a bevy of friends, especially Arthur Jones, the women of Loretto Spirituality Network, Klarise Davis and Marlene Weissshaar, who helped in the birthing of *Roots and Wings*.

I apologize for the sexist language which appears in many of the quotations and excerpts from material written before consciousness was raised. The language used is part of our history.

RL

FOREWORD

After reading *Roots and Wings* I thought: "How much would I like for the reader to meet Rose Lucey, the author of this book!" Every word she writes exudes her energy, her enthusiasm, her faith and her compassion. She incarnates so beautifully the ideals she expresses that knowing her would be the best way of becoming convinced of the importance of her message.

I first met Rose with her husband Dan at a CFM convention at Notre Dame University. Her openness and directness made me aware from the first moment that she would not let me go far without challenging me, calling me to better things, pushing me away from complacency and pulling me again and again to the center. Here was a woman who loved the church, but never hesitated to be critical, who cared deeply for individual people, but always kept her eyes on the global picture, who fully accepted her role as wife and mother, but persistently fought for the liberation of women, who was not ashamed of her traditional middle-class milieu, but kept opening people's eyes to the plight of the poor in her own city as well as in the Third World. Strong and compassionate, sharp and humorous, provoking and affectionate, activist and very prayerful.

Where did all the good energy come from? Rose said to me: "Dan and the Christian Family Movement, these are the two most informative influences on my life." Dan gave her a deep faithful love and a true home where she could offer space to nine children. The CFM prevented her from becoming a homebound, tired housewife and made her claim the whole world as her place. I never understood how she did it all, but Rose believed that everything was possible for someone who would claim her true vocation. With Dan she visited five continents and wrote *The Living-Loving Generation*. With him too she started the San Ysidro Shop bookstores in Canoga Park, Torrance, and Oakland, CA, even when Dan worked full time for the Post Office and Rose had nine children to care for. And as the children gradually moved out of the house her involvement in current issues increased. She joined the Board of *The National Catholic Reporter*, worked for Jubilee West in Oakland, became part of the Ecumenical Peace Institute, worked for the National Peace Academy, gave much of her time to a network of support communities in the Bay Area and struggles for women's rights with the Loretto Spirituality Network. With Dan she also started the Third Life Center to bring people up to date on what goes on in the Church and in the psychological world. She offers workshops, educational programs and brings people together who otherwise would never have met.

Does Rose have many degrees? None. Does she speak many languages? No. Does she have powerful connections in the political world or in the Church? None. Maybe a lot of money? No. Rose believed that she had a gift to share and a large world to share it with. She is a self-made woman or, I should say, a God-made woman, a woman who allowed God to give her the hope, courage and confidence to speak out and act out and thus to touch the life of many in very profound ways.

I could never be long in her presence without having to let go quickly from my self-complaints, my feelings of rejection, my low self-esteem, my moodiness and depression. She always says in some way or another: "Get moving, claim your gift, use your priesthood, be faithful, work hard, speak up, and don't waste a minute of your time."

Rose is far from naive. She has suffered too much to be naive. She knows the world of pain, not just from reading and travelling, but also from loving deeply those who are closest to her. Her children and grandchildren seem to incorporate all the pains and agonies of our contemporary world. Few issues of our day were not lived by someone close to her. Nothing remains theoretical for Rose. One of her greatest tests came when Dan died in 1983. Her grief was deep and often seemed paralyzing. But her love for Dan was stronger than her sense of loss and after a period of mourning she felt a strong call to continue her life in his spirit and to work even harder for the ideals that he had nurtured in her. Soon she was tested again. In October 1985 her son John died. Never have I seen a mother preparing her son for his death as Rose prepared John. Her loving and unwavering faith allowed her to let him go in peace and to become a source of hope for many of her son's friends. Rose truly knows life, without any romanticism or false decoration. She has tasted the full of it, but always was able to turn her sorrows into joy and to translate that joy in action for justice and peace.

It is a great joy for me to recommend this book to the reader because in it I see a strong affirmation that claiming God's gifts, trusting in the power of love and acting in faith are the ways to live a fruitful life in the midst of a power hungry world. The story of the Christian Family Movement is a true story of hope. The fact that the story is told by Rose Lucey makes it an even more powerful witness to the strength of the human spirit.

— Henri Nouwen

PROLOGUE

For forty years, members of the Christian Family Movement, using the simple book, *For Happier Families*, learned to see the Gospel as a call to action. Using the natural method of Observe-Judge-Act, designed by Canon Joseph Cardijn of Belgium, CFM produced a cadre of Christians whose actions for peace and justice cross national boundaries.

Joseph Cardijn was born on November 18, 1882 in Belgium, the son of a textile worker. He became a priest who often visited factories and learned how neglected and demoralized many young workers felt. In 1912 he founded the Young Christian Workers to work with trade unions and cooperative groups. While in prison during World War I, he reflected and wrote down the convictions he held about the mission of ordinary men and women. After the war, he became a spokesman for all lay movements in the church.

Cardijn taught that Observe-Judge-Act was needed because each person's human mission was absolutely necessary in the bringing to fruition of God's loving design. He spent his life teaching mainly lay people about the beauty and challenge of their mission. Eventually Pope John XXIII would ratify Joseph Cardinal Cardijn's insightful idea in the encyclical *Christianity and Social Progress*, noting that Observe-Judge-Act was the ideal pattern for families.

Somehow the simplicity of this approach and the dedication of CFM couples paid off. The results can be seen in the children of CFM families. They took a look at their homes, neighborhoods, parishes, communities and the world, and asked if what they saw squared with the Gospel vision and, when it didn't, these young people moved to change it.

While lamentations are heard about the lack of family education, the obvious successful model of CFM — tested, tried and true — continues to encourage and enable couples and youngsters to build happier families.

Life is to be lived. Books are read, discussion groups increase and multiply, trendy ministries develop; but life is to be *lived*. Action is the response to the call of the Gospel. Families deserve to experience the genius method of the Christian Family Movement as they grow in love, learn to see the world, evaluate needs, and act on behalf of others.

Today CFM continues to provide a launching pad into the future with its creative programs. *Love Happens in Families; The Eve of Orwell: A Christian Response to a Brave New World; In Search of Jesus; Come Thru Life with Me; Families Called to Action* are just a few.

The concept of the world as one human family and the wings given our children are a gift of the God of life. The simple method of Observe-Judge-Act of Canon Joseph Cardijn remains a model for the church of the future.

AN OPENING WORD

Forty years ago, a young priest of the Los Angeles diocese, John Coffield, asked Dan and me to a meeting held in Encino, California. We went to meet a couple from Chicago, Pat and Patty Crowley, who would talk about a new movement for families. That meeting in Encino was the open sesame to a life of wonder and grace for us.

Dan and I had been feeling like strangers in a strange land. We had moved from Massachusetts to California with our two little girls, Mary and Martha. At home we left our community of caring and supportive friends who were involved with the Catholic Worker, the budding Liturgical Movement and had opened the Pius XI Cooperative Bookstore in Boston. At the "Pixie Coop," as it was called, we propagated the works of Montcheil, Jacques and Raissa Maritain, Yves Congar, Guardini, Karl Adam, John Courtney Murray. We knew the winds of change were stirring in the Church and we wanted to be a part of the breakthrough to come with Pope John XXIII and the Second Vatican Council.

Here in California, we were lonesome newcomers yearning to find a similar community. Our quest was disheartening until the night we met Pat and Patty and heard about the Christian Family Movement.

In Encino we listened avidly as Pat and Patty described small groups of couples, together with a chaplain, coming together to search for the meaning of the Gospel in their daily lives. What intrigued us most was what they called the Social Inquiry part of the meeting. Applying the Gospel to the situations in which couples find themselves, as family, church people, citizens, using a method called Observe-Judge-Act. We knew it was what we were looking for. Soon after, we were delighted to be asked to join a CFM group in North Hollywood with Cecil and Arthur Piantadosi Marge and Dan Harland, Jack and Dorothy Wynns and Kate and Bob MacMahon.

For forty years we grew to respect the basic tenet of CFM, to Observe-Judge-Act. We took tiny steps at home to deal with family prayer, chores, meeting new neighbors and moved to take larger steps with our group. We took active part in parish activities, school meetings, in the political life of our community. Youngsters from the Rancho San Antonio Boys Home were welcome at our celebrations. Our families became partners in the work of Sister Elizabeth Prus and the Sisters of Social Service with the neighborhood people of Guadalupe Center; we invited foreign visitors to stay with us.

Recently I looked through an old Guest Book we kept during our years in Los Angeles. In that time we had entertained visitors from fifty-one countries. What an education and privilege for our own family and the other families who would join us to entertain people from Africa, Asia, Europe, South America, and the Near East.

The little yellow book, *For Happier Families*, was our primer. Over the years programs would draw us further and further to recognize the crying injustices of our age: racism, poverty, agism, sexism, the blasphemy of war. Our small circles grew. Dan and I headed the West Coast Federation of CFM and then went on to the National Executive Committee and, ultimately, the Executive Committee of the International Confederation of Christian Family Movements. At every step we met remarkable caring people, wanting to share their lives with others.

The present view I hold of our world as one family of

An Opening Word

God I owe to my experiences in CFM. As Dan and I traveled on every continent we faced the harsh realities of countless people living in abject poverty. We realized that, for some, the Christian Family Movement was imperfect, but for us, it was the prophetic voice in the church, calling us always to move further in action for justice.

The Christian Family Movement provided us the gift of beautiful friendships. From the early years we grew to know Pat and Patty, Reggie and Ralph Weissert, Bill and Laura Caldwell, Herb and Betty Springer, John and Dorothy Drish — and to love them.

Some of our children grew to be fast friends. Across the miles that separated us, we shared the trials and tribulations of family life, involvement in social action and celebrated our love for each other and our families. To this day these friends remain treasures in my life.

Roots and Wings is only an inkling of the revolution in families who joined together to bring the vernacular into the Mass, to enflesh the documents of Vatican II and Pope John XXIII's magnificent *Peace on Earth (Pacem in Terris)*.

Kay and Gary Aitchison, Executive Directors, have articulated a new challenge: "The CFM of the future must continue to arouse a concern for peace and justice, as well as more simple lifestyle in its member couples as well as in society."

The archives at the University of Notre Dame house the complete history of the dreamers and doers in the Christian Family Movement, families and religious acting together to build a better world. In the future an in-depth history of CFM will be written. *Roots and Wings* is a small beginning.

For Daniel Lucey
1915-1983
My dearest friend and companion
and our children
Mary, Martha, Ann, Christopher
Monica, John, Peter, Crista and Meira

CHAPTER I
Gifts

"There are two lasting gifts we
can give our children:
one is roots;
the other is wings."

We gave them roots.

We gave them wings.

We expected them to fly in our orbit.

We stand in awe as they soar
like young eagles into worlds
beyond our dreams.

The litany of the young who have chosen to live the Gospel imperative is long. The stories are not atypical. A whole generation captured the vision of a new world, based on love, peace and justice; who were impelled to leave their comfortable nests to soar into unknown territory. They are doctor, lawyer, chief, butcher, baker and candlestick-maker; alive, aware, questioning, educated, articulate, discerning, restless. Their small, childish world grew gradually until it surpassed the boundaries of their place. Their lives testify to the force of the idea of *For Happier Families*, a little yellow book which taught about a better life, not only for "my" family, but for all families. Young people watched their parents, participated with other CFM families in actions, and grew into caring, perceptive adults.

Meeting by meeting, step by step, families were led to see the Gospel message present in the 20th century; to see the connection between reading the Gospel and acting on it. *For Happier Families* taught the technique of Observe-Judge-Act. To take a look at a home, neighborhood, parish community; ask if what existed squared with the Gospel vision; and if not, act for change.

- Bruce is a doctor on an Indian reservation.

- Cynthia is a professor of law, working for social change. Cynthia started law school in 1969. Less than ten percent of her classmates were women. She says, "I changed a lot that year. I realized I had more than most other students in the class as far as grasping legal concepts and being able to articulate them. My concept of what is possible for women expanded."

    After graduation Cynthia practiced poverty law, then went on to teach at a prestigious school of law in 1975. She practices private law, is an Equal Opportunity Commission Hearing Officer and works with friends to organize a community shelter for middle-class women she believes are not having their needs met.

    Cynthia reflects, "The challenge for me is to find things worthwhile doing in the community. Every human being should be able to make a personal impact on society."

- Laurie is the organizer of a Women's Center at her university.

- Camy lives in the Southwest, demonstrates against nuclear weaponry, travels with her puppets preaching the gospel of peace, openness toward other cultures and awareness of the difficulties encountered by the disabled. She has lived and worked in Japan, Tanzania and Brazil. Reflecting on her work for social justice she says,

"I have a memory as a child in a CFM family of going out to the country with our used clothes for another CFM family. It appeared a peculiar kind of 'charity' as the children seemed just like my sister and me. This memory makes me laugh now, but it was a wonderful lesson in the equality of giver and receiver. No doubt this had some influence on my current life-style and values."

- Mary and Laura, a mother-daughter nurse team, work as volunteers in a poor people's health center in Cleveland which they helped organize.

- Patsy is director of a job center and low-cost housing in Chicago's inner city. She remembers visiting the "projects" when she was growing up, a world totally unlike the one in which she lived.

- Steve has seen his dream of a home for dependent boys become a reality. With the help of wife and friends, the residential facility he designed while in high school now exists in the wide-open, gracious arms of nature, in the hills of California.

- After seeing a film about a pen-pal program in which lonely senior citizens and youngsters corresponded, nine-year-old Peggy gathered sixteen friends in the Pittsburgh area to begin a similar project.

- Young Kristen and her peers wanted their own Christian Family Movement program. They wrote a book, appropriately titled *In Search of Jesus*, bringing teens through the study of Scripture and using the Observe-Judge-Act technique to find Jesus as a friend, to know their gifts and potential and to move out into the community.

- Martha volunteered as a Mission helper in rural North Carolina to experience first-hand the sin of segregation — before the civil rights days.

- Chris and Mary went to the Peace Corps, one to India, the other to Ecuador.
- Peter spent college weekends helping rehabilitate a monstrous dilapidated house to be used as a visitors' center for families of prisoners.
- Susie remembers CFM families in her parish working with others to integrate housing in their midwestern community. She reflects sadly on the prejudice and bitterness she saw. She remembers that students from a neighboring university were always welcome at the family table. They came from every part of the world and from diverse backgrounds. Dinner conversation flowed like a bubbling brook on topics of international life, economics, culture, religion, peace. Social worker and teacher, Susie's roots are in her midwestern CFM home; her wings have borne her to the barrios of Latin America.
- Bruce and Mary worked summers in a parish in East Los Angeles, teaching English and Bible classes. They also experienced the infectious joy of children and grownups who loved life, song and dance. Bruce now is a community organizer in Michigan.
- Mary lives and works south of our borders. In the slums of Actipan she learned the connection between destitution and despair; she saw life lived without basic human needs. How could she teach women to sew if there were no scissors? Broken glass was plentiful so Mary developed a method of using the glass to shear the material. It was her first experience of the poverty Dom Helder Camara describes as "misery which is revolting and degrading," a lesson she never forgot. In a poignant letter home she wrote:

"Daddy, people say Mexicans are lazy and sleep all day. You would, too, if you never had one day in your life with enough to eat. Don't let people talk like that."

Gifts

- George, Amy, Esther, Bob and Bill are only a few of the young who experienced a CFM Mission Vacation. For over 20 years, dozens of families traveled to Appalachia to share work and play with other families. In their formative years the children encountered the effects of poverty, malnourishment and lack of opportunity in their own country. In the broadening experience of repairing houses, cooking, teaching Bible classes, picnicking, dancing and storytelling, young people learned Camy's lesson of the equality of giver and receiver.

- Anne and Mary reflect on growing up in a CFM family:

    We remember a summer trip through Georgia visiting CFM groups, playing with the kids while Mom and Dad met with parents.

    A favorite time was the CFM Halloween party fun to dress as our favorite saints. In retrospect, it was great family entertainment.

    Other families and priests were always welcome at our house. We remember Dad blessing the house on January 6, the Feast of the Epiphany, the Christmas Eve nativity processions and feast day parties. Every Sunday after Mass, Mom and Dad asked us, "What was today's Gospel about?" Anne always answered, "Jesus and the Apostles." She was usually right!

    Social action was the backbone of CFM. Our family's involvement in civil rights in Tennessee in the early sixties was part of our CFM life. We had students from other countries and lonely people in to dinner. Going to the park we always had to leave it cleaner than we found it. To this day we can't walk by litter!

    The highlight of summers was the CFM Convention at Notre Dame; so much to do, so many people to meet.

    Blessed by being raised by our parents, Bill and Laura Caldwell, we know CFM was a big part of their formation as people, as a couple and as parents.

    Now we put high priorities on family activities,

involvement in our parishes, community and schools. We learned organizational skills at home, striking forward for nonviolent social change. Our family all live different life-styles, yet attempt to instill deep values in our own families, rejecting materialism and consumerism. Our ideas of family life are not a popular approach these days, but they are the best way.

Families planted deep roots in the soil of friendship by studying, praying, playing and working together. The traditions of family and church were celebrated with exuberance on birthdays, feast days and anniversaries. In the constantly extending CFM family of natural and chosen members, meeting new people and adjusting to changing situations were part of growing up. Understanding, compassion, sharing and caring were arts to be learned.

Wings were developed in group games, family camps and collective projects. Wings were tested as the young took small steps with parents to feed the hungry, clothe the naked and visit the sick. Later they would strengthen their wings as they walked with the farm workers, gathered medicine and food for migrants, taught children, welcomed refugees as their adopted brothers and sisters.

From their earliest years this privileged group of young heard the Gospel as a familiar challenge with which to grapple, a struggle with the question "How will I live my life?" Observe-Judge-Act was a yardstick for evaluating the wide spectrum of situations at home and at school.

Youngsters observed as their parents dealt with the soul-searching questions "Who is my neighbor? What is the church? What is my responsibility to the world?" They noted their mothers were equal partners in the process of discussion and decisions. They picked up information that would be questioned, sorted and catalogued for future reference.

Growing up, they struggled with demands made on them to share meals, time and even their beds, giving them up to strangers. Being friendly to kids in trouble was a strain, seeking ways to relate to students and visitors from foreign lands was a burden. Sharing did not come easy for young people whose contemporaries were experiencing life quite differently. In spite of extraordinary privileges and the support of the larger community of CFMers, feelings of frustration surged over them.

In a moment of honest anger, a teenage son demanded: "Why can't we be ordinary Catholics just like everyone else? Why do we always have to share? Why can't we just have our family over for Christmas dinner this year?" Demands were often hard on the young.

Consolation came from CFM peers in the gift of a quote: "Remember, life is not neat"; and from forming deep friendships.

"You have given me not only your love, sisters and brothers, friends in Ohio, California, Mexico, France and Australia, but also faith and creative insight, the real things that last and grow," wrote a young woman away from home.

Mothers and fathers share their lives, vision and work with their young for a short time. Roots go deep, wings sprout. The expectation is the young will fly in our orbit, act as we acted. Why are we surprised when this generation soars into unexplored territory, beyond our wildest expectations? Their call to life is not ours, it is a mystery that comes from beyond us. They are our guests.

The self-confidence of the young is a reflection of the love and affirmation provided by the community of the Christian Family Movement. In this school of Christian living, youngsters are encouraged to have great expectations for themselves and for the future. Life is not simple, it is a great adventure to be lived in a complex and changing world.

Reminiscing, Therese writes:

> I admit that as a child I resented growing up in a CFM home. I felt CFM stole my parents from me. Where was the normal dining room table for only two parents and their children? And who were the kids who were such great models? As I

grew older I realized we CFM kids were not perfect but good kids with human weaknesses, sharing the same unusual but loving upbringing.

I see now it is hard to let your parents go: to let them pursue their own beliefs and goals. Seeing my parents, other CFMers, their communication, joy of each other's company, involvement in family, community and the world — energy, compassion, faith and hope seem to be key words in describing them. It is hard to be objective when you are growing up.

Now I want that kind of relationship, that kind of love and devotion in my own marriage. I don't know if that kind of attitude is acceptable in our "disposable" society, but the kind of love my parents shared will live on in me.

CHAPTER II
To Tell a Story...

"There exists in the US today hundreds of families attempting to live a family-style spirituality. These families and clergy are members of CFM groups.....which have sprung up in parishes throughout the country." from CFM Peaceworks book.

It is time to tell a story of families in action. This dynamic and life-giving tale of the Christian Family Movement and its impact on the American Church and society needs to be recounted. The genius of CFM was, and is, that it answers the hunger in persons to grow and live a life of meaning and responsibility consonant with the Gospel. Born in the middle of the 20th century, this innovative model of wives and husbands working together for nonviolent social change is still vital. New generations need to know that families working, playing, studying and struggling together can bring vision into reality.

The Christian Family Movement came into being at a new moment in U.S. history. After World War II, many young married couples were moving around the country. Often they were strangers in a strange land, feeling a need for community, support and friendship. Traditional church groups were separated by gender — some for men, some for women — offering little appeal to couples. There was a realization among some Catholics that Christianity was more than inward gazing, that the Gospel message was an outward thrust.

A long-time CFMer writes:

> What were we looking for? We young marrieds of the late '40s and '50s? We were married couples, in love with each other, in love with the church. We were living in a society where mobility was a part of life. We were products of a Catholic upbringing which saw the parish as the center of life, the family as the foundation of society. We belonged to parish groups which were segregated, women from men, men from women. We longed to work together as husbands and wives. We believed there was more to life than socializing. We wanted to believe a new world could be built. We wanted "more" from our marriages and from our church, but we didn't know what.

It was in this milieu that a small group of far-sighted Catholics in mid-America designed a model for couples, families and religious to join together. Building on the pioneer experience of a group of couples begun with Father Louis Putz at Notre Dame, and fostered by Helene and Bernie Bauer, the stage for CFM was set. In Chicago and other places similar experiments were being made.

Meeting together, these pioneer couples and clergy made a decision to translate the innovative philosophy of Canon Joseph Cardijn of Belgium into contemporary American experience. The method Cardijn used in his ministry to the Young Christian Workers of Belgium (called "Jocists" from the initial letters of *Jennesse Ouviere Chretienne*), to Observe-Judge-Act, offered the pattern for families to work with families. Designed to unleash the untapped potential of the people of the Church, the pattern identified three steps to take in looking at life:

1. Get the facts
2. Evaluate the new information
3. Take action

It was a revolution in religious education and, one suspects, a forerunner of the Base Communities of Latin

America. In his book, *Tracing The Spirit* (Paulist Press), James E. Hug S.J. says: "Various approaches are being used in the attempt to trace the Spirit in social realities and movements. Some are simple and preliminary, some are developed and elaborate. They have precedents — perhaps even historical roots — in movements such as those spawned by the Jocists."

The Christian Family Movement laid the foundation of a lived theology, forming deep roots in the American Catholicism of the 20th century. It was a theology born before the days of the Vatican II. The CFM goal of educating and activating members as part of the modern world posed a challenge: it was to eliminate the gulf between the spiritual life and the so-called secular life. They are not two separate existences but one life to be lived. The families were not concerned with building a structure, they were interested in living out the call of the Gospel within their own environment.

There was a heady feeling as couples believed that their thoughts, words and actions were important in the development of the family of God. By the process of Gospel reflection, Observing-Judging-Acting, they learned it is not possible to think oneself into a new way of acting, but it is possible to act into a new way of thinking. This was an exciting insight. It is not enough to study and discuss a situation; responsible Christians must take a leap into the field of direct action, no matter how small. These practitioners of a new model of marriage, of couples acting in tandem for personal and social change, accomplished a dynamic breakthrough in the model of sacramental marriage. The unprecedented model intrigued the laity and clergy.

Pat and Patty Crowley of Chicago became the first Executive Secretary couple of CFM and the formative text used for CFM, *For Happier Families*, affectionately called 'the little yellow book,' has been used by thousands of couples throughout the world.

Patty Crowley remembers the first edition of *For Happier Families* was published on May 16, 1949. It was gray and turned yellow on November 30, 1952. In the first years of CFM, all correspondence and work was done around the dining room table at the Crowleys' in Elmwood, Illinois. "After-convention" parties were also held at the Crowleys'. One year, thirty-two CFMers arrived and stayed overnight, filling up every available room and all the floorspace.

The first issue of *ACT* was October, 1946. From 1953, Pat's law office address was used, though the work continued at the house.

In May of 1962, the Christian Family Movement office moved to 1655 W. Jackson St. in Chicago, where it remained until October, 1977. When Pat and Patty Crowley resigned as president-couple in 1970, Cathy and Bob Burggraf became the new couple. Cathy died one year later, leaving behind memories of love and cheerfulness and willingness to keep the office alive. In 1971, Ray and Dorothy Maldoon were elected president-couple and the office was moved to 2500 New York Avenue in Whiting, Indiana. With the advent of the leadership of Kay and Gary Aitchison, the office now resides in Ames, Iowa.

The introductory process, used in groups of six couples, is simple and direct. Meetings begin with a short reflection on a Gospel passage, focusing not on its meaning in the ancient world but on what it is saying today. What does Jesus mean when He says, "I am the vine and you are the branches"? What is it, today, to ask the question of the young man: "...And who is my neighbor?" What is it for a young father in a group to venture that he has not spoken to his brother, an alcoholic, for several years? What does it mean for couples to reflect on poverty and racism in their neighborhoods? The Gospel becomes a living question through which people grapple with the requirements of living as a Christian.

The radical, demanding section of the biweekly CFM

meeting is the Social Inquiry. Through the discipline of getting facts (observing), evaluating the information (judging), and deciding on action (acting), couples address issues affecting family, parish, community and nation. Simple, beginning steps are to reach out to neighbors, deepen prayer life, spend time with the family. But simple, beginning steps lead into larger, more complex forays into all areas of church and secular society which impinge on the family.

For Happier Families was first published in 1949, to influence two generations. Since the 1950s, yearly programs of CFM have covered tremendously broad subjects: Building Community; *Mater et Magistra*; Parish and Community; Race and Social Harmony; *Pacem in Terris*; The Changing Liturgy; Shalom; Work, Money, and Your Family; Challenge to Change; Quality of Life; The Family in a Time of Revolution; Ministering Together; Come thru Life With Me; The Eve of Orwell; Your Family Called to Action.

Meantime, families were actively involved in parishes and communities. Credit unions were organized on a parish level, foreign students and their American hosts melded cultures across international lines.

In Chicago, CFMers were investigating discrimination in the insurance field against black people.

While at a yearly convention at the University of Notre Dame, Frank Sheed of the prestigious publishing firm of Sheed and Ward noted he had never spoken at a convention where there was an equal number of men and women present, working together.

In the decade of the family, the 1980s, the increasingly ecumenical CFM has programmed material covering drug abuse and alcoholism, ministry to divorced and separated, fears of growing old, parenting for peace and justice, and the list continues to grow. The Christian Family Movement's School for Lived Theology has educated concerned Christians for forty years.

"Life can never be the same again," say CFMers who

have been part of the great moments of religious ferment and growth in the 20th century.

By the time of Vatican II, a worldwide network of over 100,000 action-oriented and educated laity were eager and able to integrate the call of the Council documents into their lives. Today the fundamental tenet of CFM to educate and activate is a methodology deeply embedded in the minds and hearts of Christian Family Movement couples, families, clergy and religious on every continent.

The people of the Christian Family Movement believe that every person has unlimited potential for growth and service. This belief is based on the image used by St. Paul and one which Monsignor Reynold Hillenbrand spent his life teaching to CFMers: "We are all baptized into one body, Jesus Christ." As simple as that. That belief accepted, it follows that there is no one who can say to another, "I have no need of you." By this simple, profound belief, CFMers know that their lives, stances and actions are crucial to the completion of the body of Christ in humanity.

The story of the long, exciting journey of the Christian Family Movement through unexplored territory, magic forests, slippery streams, green meadows and high mountains is the uninterrupted story of people open to the world.

CHAPTER III
To Educate and Activate

> "It is in each of us that the peace peace of the world is cast In the frontiers of our hearts From there it must spread out to the limits of the universe."
>   Cardinal Leon Joseph Suenens

The years between 1955 and 1966 were years of explosion and expansion for the Christian Family Movement in America. By 1960 there were groups in all but three states in the union. The expansion, some said, was only horizontal, not vertical enough. Others would say that developing leadership took time, that CFM was for everybody and no one was to be excluded.

Most couples came into CFM because they wanted to be part of a community and wished to make some sense of their lives. They were asked to become serious readers of the Word, to reflect on their experiences in the light of the Gospel, something unheard of in their day. This was challenge enough; yet they were also expected to do their homework in new areas which deeply affected their lives — community, politics, education, work — and for this they were ill-prepared by the church.

In the theology of the Mystical Body which Monsignor Hillenbrand drummed into our hearts and minds was a radical concept for couples. To understand we were the church, that our individual gifts were for the total family of God, was a revelation. We had to hone our learning skills as we ventured to act in the world.

To educate and activate became a goal. The exciting and demanding meetings about Family Relationships, Economic Life, Social Responsibility, Peace in the World, presented a lot of material with which to deal. Couples and their chaplains struggled together to forge a new concept of church. Growth in CFM was not automatic. We were discovering together that Gospel living was a new way of life. We were being forced to look out into the world with new eyes.

The chaplains grew with us and called us to maturity. "CFM is not a program for spiritual security," said Dennis Geaney, faithful priest and friend. Dennis did much to set the basic philosophy of understanding between priest and people. "We need to be compassionate with each other," he often said. "Christians are not to look for cozy corners, but to find the gaping wounds in human relations which need the binding love of CFM people." He also reminded us to look for the wounds in our own families and husband-wife relations. "The chaplain's role," he said, "was to be the prophet and light fires. We were not just another group, we were forging the work of a lifetime." Priests and people became fast friends as they worked side by side.

Leo Edgerly, a Deacon, and his wife, Myrtle, of St. Andrew's Parish in Oakland, both members of the Knights and Ladies of St. Peter Claver, remember being young marrieds. "I came from a Baptist background," recounts Myrtle. "In our church everyone knew everyone and there was a warm and loving feeling. I didn't feel at home in the Catholic Church until Father John Garcia got us involved in CFM. We studied Scripture and talked about what was happening in our lives. It made religion seem more real. Before this, husbands went to one thing in the church, wives to another. But in CFM we did things together, to study and talk together. It was the foundation for all the work we do now."

Leo remembers that the rounded program of CFM

engaged the whole family. He remembers being surprised when a couple in their group who had nine children said they took a day off a month to go away together.

The younger couples couldn't see leaving children at home, but we learned that, once the children leave, there is a vacuum. For me, I thought CFM was the greatest community builder ever found and can't understand why the church didn't get behind it. He goes on to say:

> Any success we've had from our family came from CFM families being and working together. It was wonderful to see couple, family and pastor working together. To have the priest drop in was great. We Catholics weren't too familiar with Scripture. I remember the first time Myrt and I decided to go away on an anniversary. It was the blossoming of a new state in our marriage. The CFM taught us to cope with change. We were ready for Vatican II because of our study of the liturgy and doing the Inquiries.
>
> Our group was special. We had blacks, Spanish-speaking, white people, Portuguese in the group. We loved each other, we had a community. If the CFM was in every parish, we'd be more of a real family now. Our chaplain, Father Garcia, was shrewd. He always said, "The Bible is something no one can be positive about." He always said, "You don't *Judge* anybody! People will grow!" I've never been afraid to reach out. You know I stammer. But Myrt and I worked together, she helped me and CFM was my stepping-stone. Because of the support and encouragement the group gave me, I am not afraid to stand up and talk to anybody. The CFM was a major tool for me.

Couples studying their environment and community learned that improvement meant people working together. The discovery of the lack of facilities for teenagers was an important issue and people were called to come together. When it became apparent through the Social Inquiry that politics was a vital individual responsibility, couples moved to join political organizations. They learned to take part in the political process and to constantly reach out to get others to join them.

As the movement grew, the network of small groups melded into federations. Larger actions could be taken hosting foreign students and visitors, for instance. Conventions could also be held, which not only provided new energy but new friendships across parochial lines. At all CFM Conventions, the families never stayed in hotels or motels. They were housed by other CFM families where the words "extended family" became a reality.

Florence and John Judge of St. Paul, Minnesota, were attracted to CFM because of the focus on a better family life, "not only for our family, but for all families." Moving through the Social Inquiries they were drawn into knowing more about their own neighborhood, the nation and the world. "The CFM," this couple says, "by focusing on action, helped put what we learned in Catholic school into practice. The year-long inquiries to study Race, Economics, Family were important. The children learned from listening and taking part in discussion and the actions." Their own enthusiasm spread as they started many groups in the Twin Cities. Florence and John remember:

> We began to view people of the world as our brothers and sisters. CFM helped open a new way of thinking, praying and living each day in God. It supported our ability to question what was happening in our lives and around us. The women were vocal and questioning. We worked eagerly for the coming of the Second Vatican Council which would bring the Church into the modern world. We were ten years ahead of what was going on.
>
> Just to spend time with Fathers Bernard Haring, Dennis Geaney, to listen to speakers like Jesuits Fichter, Thomas and others at the CFM National Convention enriched our lives. The visitors we entertained because of CFM came from many countries — students, families, business people; all increased our experience of the world as a family, working toward unity. The programs dealing with race relations, family life and sex education were vitally important.
>
> The men sacrificed their own careers in order to spread

the word of CFM. The dynamic life of the movement was a power that enabled couples to really believe in themselves as agents of change.

John Judge says the leadership training of priests and people was the greatest thing that ever happened. Couples learned to work together and the CFM training affected how we lived our lives in the marketplace. John believes the most effective CFM program was on race relations. He says it affected his life and made him more aware and more sensitive to the poor and to political realities. "We developed leaders able to ask questions and make choices," John says. "I work harder for values, want what is right. Worldly goods no longer are the main drive in my life. The great challenge, and we often failed, was to work at our best potential. Often we settled for taking food to people instead of tackling the source of hunger. CFM was magic! It was a revolution. It brought women into the church. We couples talked with our bishops and priests and told them about our lives."

The methodology of the CFM — to study the Scripture as the living Word and then look at the world to Observe — Judge — Act and help build the earth was the vital instrument that changed people's lives. It was a challenging instrument, demanding a response. It was a way of living which needed to be learned by every member of the family. Words to be a talisman through life: Observe, Judge, Act. Starting with small simple actions it gave each person confidence to change their way of looking at the world. With Scripture as a base, it opened hearts and enriched family, parish, community, national and international life. It was an integrated pursuit of Christianity: adult education leading to informed action. It has often been said that if one meets an active Christian and scratches the surface, one will usually find a person formed in the Christian Family Movement.

Pat Moriarty of South Bend, Indiana, is clear about the meaning of CFM in her community.

We learned a lot through the meetings on Politics and

International Life. In my personal life, Joe and I did something together every two weeks as a couple. We prepared the meetings together, a good beginning to strengthen our marriage.

It was good for our children to meet many others at the great conventions. Our actions in *For Happier Families* were basic and simple. We moved ahead of the structure and some of us began to be cynical. We are more Christian, less Catholic. Spirituality took a definite turn from legalism toward personhood. Chaplains changed as we did and that caused problems.

We set the pattern for openness for our children and they act differently. Because they are our children, church means something to them but not the same way as for us. They need CFM to help the groping in their own lives. CFM gave great enthusiasm to parish meetings, in the city and further on. We were a nucleus for action.

Our CFM gave great enthusiasm to parish meetings, to city involvement and education. We were a nucleus for positive action. We started credit unions which became an educational program for the whole parish and we did it without paid professionals. I will never be able to shake the social conscience developed in me through CFM. We have a community of concerned families we never had. It was CFM that always pressed us to move on to the next step. The program on race relations was the bottom line. We were ahead of the days of civil rights and either opted to act or stop. It was the first time in our community that black and white families got together. We got acquainted and met in each other's homes to know each other better. Just a few months ago I met a principal of one of our schools. We had met through interracial meetings. "Too bad," he said to me, "too bad we don't have groups like CFM now when we need them so much for our school." CFM gave leadership training to people who never would have had the opportunity. The very first question of the Yellow Book, "Who is my neighbor?" is an ongoing question in life. We learned the importance of the value of persons above things.

CFMers took risks. In Muskegon, Michigan, CFMers

risked their jobs and positions because of their involvement in the Civil Rights Movement. In Canoga Park, California, couples found housing and jobs for black families and suffered insults for their efforts. Families joined with churches and other groups to produce consciousness-raising plays like "The Other Side," which challenged audiences to see themselves, the "dominant race," as a minority in a space-age world.

In towns in the heartland of America, several CFM women ran for public office in order to raise important people-issues in local campaigns. Candidates were supported and elected as families learned through study and action that they could impact society.

We were encouraged to read about art, culture, politics, peace, automation, industrialization, and Latin America. No one could read all that was available, of course, but lives were enriched. Discussions became more serious as couples struggled to integrate the information we were getting. We were pulled out of our little worlds and narrow mentality.

Responsibility was accepted as CFMers learned to reach out beyond their own circles and join with other concerned citizens. Acting for the good of the whole was part of being a fully grown human person. The support felt by couples who met in each other's homes every two weeks enabled individuals to develop potential they didn't know they had.

Former President-couple of the St. Paul, Minneapolis, Diocese Federation, Chuck and Stella Lundquist, say their involvement with CFM led to a wide range of activities.

Chuck, a medical doctor, founded the Minnesota Physicians United for Human Life, sits on the Board of Directors of the National Human Life Center, and chairs the Battered Children Committee at St. Mary's Hospital.

Stella calls herself a full-time professional volunteer. Currently, she is president of the Corporation of Mary's Shelter, the only home for single pregnant women in a five-state area. Says Stella:

> CFM prepared me for my role as the president of Mary's Shelter. I feel confident about what I am doing. It is a fulfillment and an integration of all my past involvements. I believe if I had not been in CFM, there would not be a Mary's Shelter today.
>
> Our married children are active leaders in their churches, the effect of living in a CFM family. However, I can see they have a great need for a couple-peer support group. They are involved in the community, but, because the group does not know the Observe-Judge-Act method, they often fall on their face. CFM provided that — and still does for me.

Laura Caldwell, a registered nurse and wellness specialist in Cleveland, Ohio, remembers Monsignor Hillenbrand's great emphasis on the importance of family rituals and how enriching they were for families:

> We had to get *facts* for our meetings and we learned critical thinking. Thanks to Hilly; he pushed us into new areas and we learned from all the programs. I remember: no littering, politics, racial sit-ins in the South, integrating our town swimming pool. We made great friends, and I came to believe I was part of the Church. We shared a common bond in marriage, beyond children, not gazing at each other, but out into the world. Our children did not suffer — they prayed with us, more and better. CFM gave us a sense of the need for political savvy.

Laura says all the family members are agents for change.

> We fought for a change in the church, which greatly influenced our parish. We can never get CFM out of our system — what we learned, we still do. I am the first woman chair on our faculty senate. I didn't like the husband-wife head and heart of the family that was projected, but in practice it was not so. The pope's stand on birth control damaged CFM. I am a leader — lots because of CFM. Friends in CFM always cared. When I was sick I

only had names of CFMers to call and yet they came and helped me. We didn't know how to pray and not enough attention was given to women loving and nourishing themselves. I am grateful for CFM, for not burning out as a person and for CFM's positive effect on our children.

Bill Caldwell, administrator of a program for disabled persons, was never a church-goer or Gospel reader but in CFM the Gospel made sense.

I could tie in and learned Christ and what he was about. My favorite was the liturgy discussion — I enjoyed it. The Social Inquiry was a great teacher. For the men in CFM, engineers like myself and others, the thought process was attractive because for them, the O-J-A was natural. The Yellow Book was symbolic — like the flag. Hilly (Monsignor Hillenbrand) pushed us into heavy stuff. Strained us — it was hard work and draining. Our kids learned to relate Scripture to life. No action was too small to be worthwhile.

Pat Crowley's great wisdom influenced me a great deal. We were not well-trained enough to handle some programs. My satisfaction and the core for me was the identity we found, the effect on our family, the sense of accomplishment in being a leader, the reinforcement of our marriage. The CFM Conventions at Notre Dame and in the regions validated what we were doing and we made new friends. We were able to put flesh and bones onto our vision. I am still a Mystical Body, Vine and Branches person. These ideas are fundamental and meaningful to me now in my life. We don't see these concepts much now.

Jack and Audrey Sullivan, President-couple of the Chicago Federation, recall that the rewarding things from the basic Yellow Book was to see people grow and change.

One of the outstanding attractions to the "book" was couple activities. You would discuss subjects on different levels such as the family and what you got out of the family. Nothing else offered that. It might have been a great meeting, but the best of it was when the couples would go home and discuss for hours particular aspects of the meeting. They communicated, which is rare. At the time of joining CFM, we had been married for three years and were just settling down.

The Race Relations inquiries were the greatest challenge. Many people dropped out of CFM; they didn't want to discuss it. The most significant stand in the race issue was in Chicago. A lot of CFMers were involved in the Martin Luther King Jr. marches. The strongest response was drawing people in, not just CFMers, and getting on the line. That was the strongest response, not just with words, but doing something. Yet, even those who left, at least they took a stand. Audrey was never interested in parish organizations, but because of CFM she took a different view and got involved. When changes in the church happened, CFMers made it easier for the priests. The right to help in changes was legitimatized because of supporting other organizations. CFM died for a few years because of the race issue but we got it going again.

Audrey and Jack remember how the Vietnam War and other battles affected CFM:

We were thought of as being crazy. First we were "nigger lovers" and now we were "unpatriotic" for speaking out against the war. We took a stand. It was a time of great turmoil, struggling with confusion in families, in the church. We became more mature about prayer. Action is prayer — you act according to your faith.

We wanted to feed the hungry of the world, solve the racial problem, end war, but CFM couldn't deal with all that in small or large groups; too many battles were lost. The birth control issue lost on the battlefield and great discouragement set in when justice work stopped in Chicago, but we don't want to discourage the young, new CFMers who are seeing a different day.

We are old and battle-weary and afraid of discouraging the new ones or their ideas. We are holding a group now. It might take another generation to see the possibilities and move forward again. We have to wait until the church and society can absorb more changes.

When Charles Fischer read a sociologist's prediction of a gloomy future for CFM, he wrote:

> I can't help but speculate on a vital dimension that seems to be omitted from the general picture. That dimension is CFM as a preliminary formation process and what has happened to CFMers of the past: where are they now and what are they doing.
>
> My wife, Kerry, and I became chapter members of the Sheboygan, Wisconsin, group in 1958. At the time, I was a news reporter for the Sheboygan Press and we had two children.
>
> In looking back, my wife and I can see clearly that active involvement in CFM changed our lives dramatically. We were typical young parents struggling along with our own problems when CFM opened up for us that beautiful concept we now know as commitment.
>
> I do not hesitate in saying we never would have been ready or able to follow through as Christians if we had not had the formation that CFM provided.
>
> We went on to have three more children of our own. Later we adopted a family of nine children who suddenly became orphans, making a family of fourteen children, aged (at that time) from one to thirteen.
>
> Involvement in local social concerns led to politics which led to a job as a congressional assistant in Washington...
>
> We dropped out of CFM in 1965 with a sure knowledge that CFM had done its job (for us). We looked on CFM as a vehicle of formation, which, when ripe, enabled CFMers to move on in the Christian struggle.

Vernie Dale is one of the "new, young ones." Her story is illuminating:

> I was very pre-Vatican II when we joined CFM. We had been in our parish for two years and no one called or invited us to join a group. A young man came collecting for the Dad's Club and asked us to come to a CFM meeting. It was Jerry Gillespie who said, "Come, follow me." He was killed during a robbery in October of 1983, leaving four children

and a wife.

Observe-Judge-Act is a good way to organize information and make a decision. My favorite book is *Discovering Christ*. For the first time, I really understood the Gospel was real. My decision to enroll in the pastoral ministry program at Marygrove College was influenced from the book. We've shared important things, usually reserved for families with our CFM friends. We talk about matters of deep importance, not just the "safe subjects" of weather, work, kids, latest news, books, movies. We talk about human concerns like death, aging, stages of our marriage, homosexuality, church, Jesus. There is a freeing spirit in finding other couples who listen and are concerned.

I've accepted myself as a person. There is no such thing as a perfect wife, marriage, family. We are all imperfect — all learned through our CFM experience. We have learned we can run meetings, address large audiences, that we have something to contribute, we all do.

I have changed my perception of church and am now involved and committed in my parish. CFMers are among the most informed couples we know, who subscribe to Catholic periodicals, stay updated on the future of the church, quietly offer religious education, work in soup kitchens and among the poor in Appalachia and raise children to be aware of peace and justice on a global scale.

CFM doesn't realize how radical and prophetic it is. Theologians and the Pope are now speaking out about God incarnate in the family process — something CFM has known since the beginning. The unique success of CFM is thinking in an alternative way about minority groups and women and knowing there is room for discussion.

The great vehicle designed by Canon Cardijn was the Inquiry method; to Educate and Activate. Monsignor Hillenbrand urged all who would listen to understand the method more fully, see the possibilities in it and use it to move from discussion into action. "The Inquiry probes into our problems and, therefore, probes into life and keeps the whole thing realistic," he would say. "If people congratulate you on the fact that you are ordinary people, not dilettantes, not people up in the clouds, that isn't due only to the fact you happen to be people like that by nature. It is because the movement has reinforced that in you. It has made you more realistic, more genuine because it so strictly rooted you in the problem of the Inquiry, week after week, month after month, year after year." It was a message he never ceased repeating. It was the method that continues to educate and activate the children of the original CFMers and the growing number of families who search for a community of faith which calls them to see their home unit as a nourishing place for the gifts to be shared with the whole human family.

Affirmation came from Coadjutor Bishop James W. Montgomery of Chicago when, in the second printing of an Episcopalian edition of *For Happier Families*, he wrote in the preface:

> Two of the most significant movements of Christianity in our time are concerned with the role of the laity and with reunion — the Ecumenical movement.
>
> The Church's witness in the world required that men and women not be passive hearers of the Gospel message, mere spectators of the dreams of redemption, but active, intelligent, enthusiastic sharers in the task of making Christ known to all people.
>
> The work of translating the teaching of our Faith into the substance of the realities of our Christian vocation requires cooperation of clergy and laity on every level. One of the finest methods is the Christian Family Movement, pioneered by the Roman Communion and tested by many years of responsive growth. It is surely a symbol of the growing bonds of unity between Christians that we share in the CFM program, adapted to our own Anglican ethos and expressing our own formularies and authorities.
>
> We are grateful to the CFM for their aid and encouragement.

CHAPTER IV
Companions on the Way

> A community learns how to laugh at its foibles, takes time to relax, play, recreate its humanity, evaluate its needs and its unique direction. Most CFMers look upon one another as friends and allies and look upon the movement as a source of education, information, formation, support and encouragement.
>
> from *Quality of Life*

Friendship is a mark of the Christian Family Movement and companions cherished. The Crowleys have been friends on the way to thousands of CFMers, crossing national and cultural boundaries as they traversed the globe, preaching the gospel of CFM. Blessed with a strong and unshakable faith, they lived what they believed.

Pat, who died on November 20, 1974, was a brilliant, wise lover of people and an eternal optimist. Graduate of Notre Dame University, citizen of the world, master diplomat, he was also a scholar. In any crisis, when tempers were at the sizzling point, he would interject a humorous tidbit, unrelated in any way to the subject, which would restore balance to the gyrating discussion.

This charismatic leader and friend of thousands died in his home amidst his family. In his last weeks of life, he was visited by many of his immense extended family and a legion of friends. Ray and Dorothy Maldoon, Executive Couple for

CFM in the '70s, said at Pat's death: "The most unique characteristic of the Christian Family Movement reflects Pat Crowley's personality as exemplar of the lay person — guided but not dominated by the clergy, enlightened but not directed by the professional."

The memorial card designed by his family was simple and direct:

> Patrick Crowley
> Born September 23, 1911
> Returned to his Lord
> November 20, 1974
>
> Husband, Father and Friend
> Whose love extended so far
> Whose faith strengthened so
> many whose hope radiated
> to all.
>
> We share his favorite
> Irish wish with you:
>
> May the road rise to meet you
> May the wind be ever at your back
> May the good Lord ever keep you
> In the hollow of His Hand
> May your heart be as warm as your hearthstone
> And when you come to die
> may the wail of the poor
> be the only sorrow you'll leave behind.
> May God bless you always.

Patty, secure, thoughtful, mother and confidante to all in need, student and citizen, graduated from Trinity College. She was the perfect foil for Pat. Patty laughed at his witticisms and was his speech-making partner. Given the honorific title of "Mr. and Mrs. CFM," they were a symbol and model of Christians in the modern world. Their favorite topic was the family; religious and community working together for justice.

Traveling on five continents, they scattered copies of

the famous Yellow Book, establishing CFM, like modern-day Johnny Appleseeds.

With Monsignor Reynold Hillenbrand, Rector of the Mundelein Seminary, this creative triumvirate turned the U.S. Church onto a new path. Monsignor Hillenbrand held his own dream of a future church, based on the doctrine of the Mystical Body, and believed in the radical approach of the Observe-Judge-Act method to change the unjust structures of society. A man with a massive mind and vision solidly based on theological precepts, he moved to construct a solid, practical program for living, which he enunciated for two decades to clergy, religious and laity who went to the CFM Conventions at the University of Notre Dame.

Not a great orator, this National Chaplain spoke with passion and conviction. He touched the center of each person's being as he talked about the Body of Christ in the world. His ability to articulate that vision turned lives around and upside down. Life could never be the same after hearing him say, "This is a tremendous unity, a tremendous oneness in which we have constantly to grow. Christ doesn't want just our money, doesn't want us just as factotums for the pastor getting things done in the parish. We are the hands and feet of Christ. Where we go, Christ goes."

He spoke with deep feeling about the wonder that priests felt as they came into contact with CFM. He told of a director of Catholic Charities who had climbed three flights of stairs in a tenement in the inner city to attend a CFM meeting, who never ceased to marvel at seeing the church in action in a small group of grassroots people, probing the Gospel and their problems.

Realist that Monsignor was, he knew moving people was not an easy task. "This isn't accomplished overnight," he would say. "It isn't done by one talk or by what a chaplain might say, or by one evening of recollection. It is going to be the persistent work over time until gradually people will see this identification with Christ. The genius of our movement is that we have cut through the knot of getting to the *people* who are so important to the oneness of Christ."

We learned from Monsignor Hillenbrand to read the morning paper with a prayerful heart and mind. He asked us to enter into the suffering of people and nations and to pray with them in solidarity as brothers and sisters. The news took on a power to move us into petition for the suffering, gratitude for the good news.

I remember vividly the Mass which Monsignor Hillenbrand celebrated the day after Marilyn Monroe died. We were upstairs, in a small room, in an old church in Chicago. He talked, at the homily, on his favorite subject, the Mystical Body. Then, this man who was always uneasy in the presence of women, often uncomfortable with couples, surprised us by saying about Marilyn Monroe words I've never forgotten: "Remember," he said, "she will not be judged as you will be judged."

Louis Putz, Holy Cross Father, Rector of Moreau Seminary, was friend and mentor to the CFMers on the Notre Dame campus, in South Bend, Indiana, and wherever he went. He propagated the Cardijn design as he traveled, teaching, preaching, challenging, encouraging people to assume their rightful position in the church. In the schools he visited he encouraged the students to gather in small groups to use the method of Observe-Judge-Act in their own lives as students.

Father Putz was instrumental in involving a dynamic nun, Sister "Gertie Joe" as she was called (now Dody Donnelly) with the Young Christian Students and the CFMers. Trusting the kids and couples to reach beyond themselves, she used her gifts of love and good cheer to challenge them to the greater questions of justice and peace. We called her a "chaplain." We had no word for a woman in that role, something we dare smile about now! Sr. Gertie Joe and Fr. Putz, two believers in people, developed a solid group of students and couples who dared step outside the boundaries of a closed society.

In East Los Angeles, a devoted young priest, John

Coffield, started CFM after meeting with Pat and Patty. Padre Juan, as this companero came to be called, helped young Mexican-American families study the Gospel and take charge of their neighborhoods. He remembers "the Sunday meeting we had in the little hall behind our church. Bishop Manning came. I remember the priest from Germany who was sour because the meetings he attended in the U.S. were well-to-do. He came to one of our meetings and was sold on CFM and took it back to the poor of Berlin."

Padre Juan remembers much more:

> Oh, those CFM Conventions at Notre Dame! So much more inspiring and renewing of my priesthood than my annual priests' retreat. One of the great things the movement taught me as a priest was a taste of family life and the privilege of parenting. The love of the movement for the liturgy fitted in with one of my deepest loves. The emphasis was right on target, so far ahead of the official Church. We felt we were leading the way to a renewal of the Church. While many saw us as radicals, we proved to be centralists, right at the heart of Christ.
>
> Before CFM I was so discouraged with losing the youth. They would succumb to the pull of delinquent gangs. With CFM things began to happen: sports, teams, clubs were started by the couples. From despair to joy.
>
> Today, I don't feel a person is a full Christian, much less a formed leader, without the training in action on the social teaching that CFM was given. The type of community CFM formed was not a hold-my-hand, stroke-me one, but an effective serving and caring one.
>
> If one of our basic moral values is find the Lord in the poor, then CFM trained us in that, little talk and thinking and lots of action.

John Coffield, the people's priest, spent his retirement years working with the illegal refugees entering the country from Mexico. Going to the border at midnight, he sought out families huddled in caves in order to minister to them. He was, is, the giant among the priests of California; a model for the eager young priests of the '50s who learned to do the works of mercy. His great heart is full of love for the poor and the disenfranchised.

Every year CFMers who made the trek to the Notre Dame Convention were exposed to and encouraged by some of the great minds of the church. Jesuit Joe Fichter challenged us to understand that "we live in the most dynamic culture the world has ever produced," that "perhaps change itself is the most important thing we have to get used to." Sidney Callahan, Father John L. McKenzie, Senator Mark Hatfield, Cleveland Mayor Carl Stokes, Elizabeth McAllister, Henri Nouwen, Clarence Rivers and Archbishop Rummel were only a handful of the speakers who challenged us to stretch our minds.

Father Bernard Haring spoke to us as peers, saying:

> Christian adulthood means one is not under the law, and yet not lawless either, but within the law of God, the law of love. To learn this law is to learn initiative, to be watchful and to grasp the opportunities to do good and bring joy; it is to recognize God's movement.... If you educate your children to this adulthood, to the spirit of spontaneity, of initiative, then you have formed apostles, men and women who will be aware of the great challenges God gives us in our time...
>
> The family is an environment of love...it is a divine enrollment only if we open our horizons to the worldwide love of Christ. We are interested in the misery of all people, if we strive together toward a solution of the great social problems of the world.

Eugene McCarthy, senator from Minnesota, candidate for the presidency, reminded us: "Politics is the art of the possible." He told us the Christian politician is not necessarily the one who is seen most often at public religious activities or conferring with religious leaders, nor the one who most vociferously proclaims his or her position as the Christian one. "The Christian in politics should be judged by the standard of whether through his or her decisions and actions the cause of justice has been advanced."

No students were more avid and interested than the CFMers, who saw the Christian Family Movement as a life-long University of Living.

We listened attentively to Father John Munier of San Francisco:

> We talk a lot about giving good example, but that term is too limited. Our very living creates a kind of air which others breathe in. All of us, not just the big names in history, contribute to the community air of our time. War, concentration camps, racial injustices, labor slavery, people with no homes, buried in prison for their beliefs, none of these are the work of one person. These are the result of group action. Part of the responsibility may be with us, if only because we have not worked hard enough to start the counter-thinking to purify the air.

The words were rooted in CFM lives. From the base of neighborhood and parish, CFMers moved from having friendly potlucks to larger actions. Countless families hosted students from other lands, adopted children of all races, sponsored refugees from Hungary, Cuba, Indonesia, Vietnam and El Salvador.

The Carotas were a familiar and famous family. Mario worked in the University of California Radiation Laboratory, but gave up his job when he became aware of the implications of his work. Mario and Estelle, with six children of their own, added twelve adopted youngsters judged "unadoptable" by the authorities. With their family and the help of friends, the Carotas built a great home for themselves and visitors on a farm in Aptos, California.

Not satisfied with only taking care of their family, Mario and Estelle's philosophy was to reach out to help the disadvantaged. Traveling in an old school bus, this CFM family traversed the road from California to Mexico many times. Like a Pied Piper, Mario gathered helpers along the way. Together with Pat and Lupe Ramirez, Ernest and

Elizabeth Johnson, Father John Garcia, this group of pilgrims helped Father Francis Marin, S.J. chaplain of the Movimiento Familiar Christiano, build a new trade school.

The bulk of funds for the expedition was raised by the Mexican community of California who sponsored spaghetti dinners and picnics, using the proceeds to buy materials and equipment.

In Mexico, the families worked nine hours a day, except Sunday, when sightseeing and picnics were arranged by the grateful Mexican people. Children helped as much as possible. Fifty school chairs were built by the group for the new facility.

Mario would exhort people:

> Go abroad without the aid of government or corporations. God provides, despite sickness, hardships and differences in personalities. American families can work together for the good of others and the love of God. We are an example for our children by being allowed to work to help others. Learn about another culture and bring back to CFM and the country a new sense and value of generosity, hospitality and enthusiasm. There is a great value in the exchange of families to break down barriers; the power of children to establish peace in the world.

On a "reverse mission program," forty students from Mexico traveled to Fowler, California, a small farming community, to help build a new church.

Peace was a deep concern of the Carota family. During the Vietnam War, Mario, Estelle, and other members of the family stood in the courts with their sons who chose to be Conscientious Objectors.

From Southern California, Herb and Betty Springer, with CFM groups in the San Fernando Valley, organized a brigade to drive a caravan of trucks filled with food, clothing, and furniture to orphanages in Tijuana, Mexico. The well-fed, well-housed Valleyites were shocked to see the crowded, crudely constructed shacks. Built by the boys in the orphanages, the buildings were open to the cold air.

Families were conscious of the devotion given the children by the Sisters and laywomen at the orphanages.

Connecting with Project Amigos of the National Council of Churches in San Diego, the traveling band of CFMers organized work parties with students from the Newman Center at the Northridge campus and the Young Christian Workers. Adult clothing was bartered with local laborers for a day's work and the new orphanages of LaCuna and El Colegio de Jesus Rougier were built.

Six Dallas families worked with the Movimiento Familiar Christiano people in Mesquital "four hours and five hundred years away from civilization as we know it." The families worked in the dispensary, in the bazaar of used clothing, and trudged through the mountains to meet people "in pitiful poverty." The couples learned how bad it was not to know Spanish. On their return, four families began to work in the slums of Dallas.

Pat and Patty Pattin started a network of CFM families concerned with mentally disabled children. Pat, an airline pilot, visited many cities and tracked down as many CFMers as he could to talk about his concern for his own daughter and other children and their families. A small article in *ACT* brought an overwhelming response. "We received letters from all parts of the U.S. and Canada from couples who share, with us, this problem. Because CFM is a family apostolate and retardation profoundly affects family, we CFMers should be the best informed members of our communities on this subject." The net result was a special inquiry in the CFM program and workshops at the CFM Conventions.

Credit unions, libraries and youth centers were formed. Women and men joined political action groups and ran for office. In Portland, Oregon, CFM leader Bill McCoy was the first black man elected to the Oregon legislature. He is now state senator, a position he has held for many years. Gladys McCoy has served on the School Board, ran for City Council and is chairperson of the Multnomah County Board of Commissioners. Other CFMers assumed office in the legislatures of Hawaii, New Jersey, Illinois, Indiana and New York. Political know-how was sharpened as families learned to work the precincts during elections promoting their special candidates.

The immense problems of migrant farm workers and their families became a matter of national CFM concern. In Tucson, Phoenix and Scottsdale, Arizona, couples worked with a trailer priest in the migrant camps. In Lake County, Indiana, CFMers set about getting federal funds for a migrant-family program. Milk and food were for the bodies of the children and for their minds, remedial education was provided.

Resentful farmers became partners with these CFMers as they installed sanitary equipment, showers and screens. Continuing relationships were developed over the years. Ray and Dorothy Maldoon, indefatigable heralds, listened to CFM children as each spring they asked, "Are we going to have a migrant program again and see our friends?" In California, CFM families joined the long march from Salinas to Sacramento, seeking farm workers' rights, seeing firsthand the structures that needed to be changed. In Saginaw, Michigan, a medical program to provide immunization and TB tests and a day school with hot lunches for a hundred children were organized with the help of seminarians, nurses, a doctor and the Young Christian Students.

In Redondo Beach, CFMers gathered truckloads of clothing for the poor in Mexicali and helped build and furnish a school for the youngsters. In Alexandria, Virginia, and Greensboro, North Carolina, CFMers established a tutoring service for black children transferring to previously all-white schools by contacting nearby colleges and other churches for assistance.

At a PTA meeting in Evanston, Illinois, John and Dorothy Drish heard a talk by the chaplain of Cook County Jail. Touched by the fact that men drift back into crime because they can't find jobs, these creative CFM leaders gathered friends and strangers to form the Citizens' Committee for Employment, which included key leaders of business, labor, government and social welfare groups. Greeted with skepticism, the committee grew to be a reforming agency in the Cook County Jail. Dorothy says, "If it hadn't been for CFM, we'd probably have looked at the prisoners' problems and said, 'Interesting, but what has it to do with us?'"

Nationally known for their efforts on behalf of prisoners, John and Dorothy held important positions on the Illinois Committee of the National Council on Crime and Delinquency, on the legislative committee of the Illinois Law Enforcement Commission, on the advisory board of the Illinois Academy of Criminology.

This admirable CFM couple brought many children into their home, adding to their own family of six youngsters. Foreign students were welcomed, as well as forty-nine foster children. The Drishes were recipients of the Illinois Governor's Justice Award in 1972 and the Brotherhood Award from the National Conference of Christians and Jews.

The long journey of families together has provided lifelong friendships. As one couple mentioned, "We have seen community leaders formed, marriages made rich and family life strong. We have seen arrogance become humility, inferiority become confidence, and hate into love. Worship, prayer and Scripture become alive where it was dormant and the church became a living reality where it held little importance before."

This was not always so as the same couple admitted: "The disappointments have been there, too — the meetings never properly prepared, actions never done, people who quit just when you most needed them. Loss of membership, the tearing down and the negative, the headaches and heartaches, the fallen idols. And yet, the positives far outweigh all of these. We have received so much more than we have been given. The CFM opened for us and many others the most important doors of our lives."

Margaret Jones, wife of Rev. Don Jones and part of the National Chaplain Team was realistic about CFM as it entered the '70s.

> Those of us who came through CFM in the '50s and '60s are oriented toward action and accomplishment, high visible caring. But as those of us who are living through the '70s realize, the way is not always clearcut. Sometimes we have to wait before we can do, frustrating for many of us who want fast results. As Christians, we can use this waiting time to develop our inner resources. It is the constant, daily, moral acts of caring which enable us to act out of the ordinary when we are called to do so. It is the Christian who cares who is able to let his or her imagination soar to the ideal, who has a sense of vision beyond the mundane, who can demonstrate the joy of personal sacrifice, the fulfillment of relationship with others. The technique and relationship of CFM unleash the ability to care in many people."

In the archives at the University of Notre Dame, more than 136 boxes of material testify to the effect of the conviction of the early pioneers, the Crowleys, Monsignor Hillenbrand, Father Putz, the Bauers, the Weisserts, the Luceys, and their followers, that the methodology of Observe-Judge-Act is a life-giving process.

The voluminous letters, the CFM magazine, ACT, federation newsletters and newspaper articles are alive with stories of famous people, church and world leaders. Most remarkable are the epistles of ordinary Christians whose lives were changed by the simple yellow book, *For Happier Families*. Companions on the way, challenging, supporting, learning, praying and acting together, the CFMers testify to the unspoken desire in every heart to truly live what they believe and to be partners with each other in seeking to build a new earth.

CHAPTER V
Stretching the Boundaries

> Remain true to yourselves, but move ever upward to greater consciousness and greater love! At the summit you will find yourselves united with all those who, from every direction, have made the same ascent. For everything that rises must converge.
>
> Teilhard de Chardin

Members of the Christian Family Movement reached maturity as actions grew in depth and scope. The elan of the couples was contagious. The Foundation for International Cooperation, Christian Family Movement Vacations, Marriage Encounter, Foreign Student Program, Movimiento Familiar and the International Confederation of Christian Family Movements scrambled the alphabet into FIC, CFMMV, ME, FSP, MFR and ICCFM. Action with and for the family, political life, workers, international life, and interfaith dialogues developed into long-range commitments. The yearly Convention at the University of Notre Dame grew like Topsy as the campus became a mecca for families studying, playing, praying, singing and dancing, pulled into a world of unexpected riches.

Foreign Student Programs in the United States during the '60s involved 50,000 students from other countries studying in American colleges and universities. They came from every continent; some of them, like Julius Nyerere of Tanzania, would become the future leaders of their countries. Alert to this parade of young people away from home and friends, simple CFM actions of invitations to the students to join families for a simple meal, grew into invitations to stay a weekend, a semester, a year with CFM families. Children learned new languages. Unusual family customs and national dishes appeared in American homes, eagerly presented by young visitors.

In parishes and neighborhoods, international festivals blossomed as students shared native dances, music, crafts, art and exotic foods with a growing circle of friends. Life-long friendships were born, to pass from generation to generation. When Patty Crowley celebrated her 70th birthday in 1983, former students who had called her "Mom" came with their children to sing her praise — some from Africa and Europe.

However, study in America was not an unmixed blessing, as Chicago columnist Jack Mabley noted:

> The students are in summer recess and they would like to eat. Some are wealthy, some don't have fifty cents in their pockets. All have one thing in common: they are bright, hardworking, ambitious, well-educated and the cream of their countries. Were they to choose Russia for their education, they would get a welcoming committee at the airport, fine housing, food and an abundance of propaganda to take back to their native lands. But they chose America. I have yet to hear one of them complain or regret the choice, but I shudder at the treatment those who are colored found in our segregation the day they landed in America.

Some of the students were ostracized, others taken into homes and made part of the family. Observing the students' financial straits, Chicago CFMers opened a job office for Foreign Students.

From India came a typical letter: "I am glad to say friends changed my impression of family life in the United

States. They beautified my image of the family and people of America. Besides, I am gratified to some extent I could clarify and improve their impression of my country. My thanks to the CFM families who made contacts for me and took me into their homes."

In 1974, when the International Confederation of Christian Family Movements wanted to meet in a developing country during the International Year of the Family, it was President Julius Nyerere of Tanzania, a former student-visitor at the Crowleys', who issued an invitation to meet in Africa.

The sense of an international family expanded when CFMers organized the Foundation for International Cooperation in the '60s. Jesuit Robert Bosc of the La Vie Nouvelle in Paris attended a CFM Convention at Notre Dame and dreamed of visits between French and American family group members to foster peace and understanding. The idea ignited some CFMers into action and a first trip to France was planned. Pere Bosc and the Mignons of Paris agreed that serious study of the language, customs and history of France was a prerequisite for the expedition.

The historic first trip was magnificent. One hundred Americans from the Christian Family Movement met in groups to study and plan for their trip. They were met on their arrival in Paris by La Vie Nouvelle families and were taken to private homes. For the French, opening their houses to strangers was a novel experience. "We thought," said one couple, "having an American husband and wife in our home would be a distasteful experience. It was a joy, it opened our whole family to a new view of America — it gave us American friends."

Couples and their hosts visited the Secretariat for Christian Unity, urban districts, worker priests, a still-operating medieval hospital, the Berliet truck and bus factory and the monks at Taize. Study seminars prepared for the Americans included discussion of marriage preparation, family movements, liturgy, school, labor, social security, economics and an outline of French foreign policy.

A year later the visit was reciprocated as French couples came for an inside view of the United States, visiting eight cities and staying with CFM families. In Chicago they visited St. Carthage Parish on the South Side. Father John Hayes was delighted: "Your visit, French and CFM people, has been a great event in our parish. What struck me was that for the first time in their life ninety-five percent of our parishioners found themselves among a large number of white people who bear no prejudice."

The international forays multiplied and the Foundation for International Cooperation became a separate entity, closely tied to CFM. Groups formed to continue the serious study of international life and the languages, customs, politics and economies of many countries. The FIC trips have included stops in Japan, Taiwan, Hong Kong, the Philippines, Italy, Ireland, France, Belgium and England. Visiting couples have lived with professionals, laborers, ardent Catholics and unbelievers. Their bond: a mutual desire to build a world of cooperation, friendship, unity and peace.

Ned and Louis Taylor, FIC enthusiasts, hosted guest families and students. Traveling to the Philippines, they were struck by the poverty of families unable to find work. In a leap of faith, they abandoned a career of financial security, beginning a small business, World Imports. With the cooperation and advice of a group of European nuns, they set up neighborhood cottage industries in Manila where families could gather to produce native crafts. At first, World Imports operated with a group of CFM volunteers. The philosophy underlying this unique commercial enterprise was to help people to help themselves. World Imports provided a market for native handicrafts for which the people were paid a just wage. As World Imports grew, contacts were made with religious and lay people groups in Mexico, Haiti, and India. With his suitcase full of samples, Ned traveled up and down the California countryside to drum up orders for the new business. His honest persuasion brought World Imports a bevy of faithful customers, many of whom appreciated his philosophy of helping people to help themselves. World Imports is a model of the personal involvement that combines economics and creativity.

Christian Family Movement Mission Vacations

While CFMers traveled abroad, others traveled as missioners in their own land. Franciscan Jude Mili of Morgantown offered CFMers an opportunity to spend vacation time in Appalachia working with families. The modest invitation caught the imagination of a few families who began the trek to what one CFMer called "No Priestland, U.S.A." The returning families told stories of the good times they had, the people they met in their groups and in telling of their adventures in ACT, the CFM magazine, the Christian Family Movement Mission Vacation was born.

Come summer, families packed their gear, took along student "family helpers" and found their way into America's hinterland. Pioneers, the Uttich and Strenski families went to St. Christopher Parish in Claxton, Georgia. They met hospitable people, visited and held workshops while their children played with other young ones, seeing firsthand the problems facing the church and families.

The Massuras, with their three boys and high-schooler Pat Baldwin, journeyed to Barbourville, Kentucky to help build a brick structure at St. Gregory's Parish. Pastor Ray Mulhern (and his dog, Mona) worked with the men and a crew of teenagers from Chicago unloading donated building supplies. Daytime was for working, evenings for storytelling and visiting.

The following summer the Wohlers, Cummings and Fishers joined the Massuras at St. Gregory's. Mary remembers Bob Wohler fell asleep in the bathtub after a hard day of construction work, a tale now part of the folklore of CFMMV. The women and older children helped Betty

Hollinde in the parish "store" selling clothing for which no money was exchanged. Using St. Gregory "charge cards," payment was made by serving hours at the parish "store."

The families saw the other side of America as they trudged through the "hollers" taking census. It was an education by experience. Discovering a single mother with a great garden, the women suggested she sell her produce to passing customers. She said she couldn't, "I don't know how to give people change."

Three families worked with Glenmary pastor August Guppenberger in Franklin, Kentucky, readying a chapel and social center for residents of the farming area. Others set out for St. Boniface Church in Jellico, Kentucky, to establish a medical clinic in the church house. Visiting with coal miners, socializing with young people from the "hollers" and driving on rutted dirt roads was an education no school could provide for CFMMV families.

A tiny acorn planted in the first small CFM action for a Mission Vacation grew into a healthy tree as the Gorciaks of Los Angeles, Paul and Irene Nathe and the O'Rourkes in Ridgewood, New Jersey, organized the family caravans to Missionland each year.

Bill and Barbara Furlong, their children and a teenager were among forty-five families who vacationed one summer in Appalachia and the South. The Furlongs cannot forget "the astonishment on an eleven-year-old's face seeing the first birthday cake of his life; the joy of fifty children having all the lemonade and hot dogs they could consume; the hopelessness of two girls crippled by polio, living in a lonely mountain cabin; the sorrow of families engulfed in poverty."

Their family went home, "physically tired out but spiritually enriched....Our children learned mountain children are no different than themselves, despite lack of material wealth. They learned little ways to give of themselves, hopefully preparing them to give in bigger ways as they mature."

La Leche League

Kathleen Miller of Mount Prospect, Illinois, remembers discussions about breastfeeding babies, not a popular or encouraged process in the '50 and '60s. Nothing daunted, a group of CFM women, with the encouragement of their husbands, joined to form the La Leche League, now an International Association. The avante-garde group included Mary White, Edwina Froehlich, Viola Lennon, Marian Tompson, and Betty Wagner. From this simple action, thousands of women around the world are able to connect with other women and doctors interested in returning this most basic gift a mother gives to her child.

Carol Ann remembers venturing to the apartment-house swimming pool and nursing her baby. "How far we've come," she smiles, "the other women at the pool called me a hussy!"

Marriage Encounter

The "special" actions of CFM broadened. In 1967, Father Gabriel Calvo of Spain presented a Marriage Encounter to the CFM Coordinating Committee meeting at Notre Dame. It was a way to involve husbands and wives in honest and loving confrontation. This meeting of CFM couples with Father Calvo was the beginning of the Marriage Encounter Movement in the United States. Couples listened to the friendly Jesuit as he told his own story. Traumatized at sixteen by the suicide of his dearest friend, Calvo struggled with the question: "How can I best help families?" He decided to enter the Society of Jesus and started working closely and intimately with couples, seeing firsthand the lack of communication and honest confrontation in some homes. From this experience he developed the model of the Marriage Encounter, providing a process for deeper openness and dialogue between spouses.

Jerry and Joan remember being present at the first Encounter.

We had been CFMers for five years, made a Cursillo, a very intense spiritual retreat, thought we knew 'all about' bringing Christ into our lives and others'. We listened to a couple recount their experience in the Encounter and working with Father Calvo. Afterwards we were given an intimate questionnaire, to be filled out, alone, with complete honesty. We were painfully honest — playing the game to the hilt, expressing our real feeling about marriage, our spouse and then, risking sharing our answers with each other. We confided to each other things we mistakenly thought we could never discuss, in a spirit of love and acceptance. By the end of the day we felt we had discovered each other for the first time. Our minds and hearts stood naked before each other. The Marriage Encounter team merely set the climate for us and the ground rules — we gave to each other by honestly facing ourselves and our marriage. It was earth-shaking for us to realize the only thing our children can hold onto is the love that exists between their mother and father.

Father Calvo's Marriage Encounter model appeared at a time when traditional marriage and family mores were under attack. The signs of the times, of parents threatened by the fast pace of social change, were flashing madly in huge neon lights but were not acknowledged. Couples wanted and needed a technique for laying a deeper foundation for their love and commitment; a way to articulate their unexpressed hopes, dreams, loves, fears, anger. The Marriage Encounter came as a gift.

Local CFM groups sponsored Encounters in Michigan, Ohio, Illinois, Texas and Washington, D.C. Father Calvo worked with an increasing number of CFM couples and chaplains who devoted more and more energy to the development and promotion of the National Marriage Encounter, siphoning off dedicated couples from CFM activity.

Movimiento Familiar Christiano and CFM Around the World

A happy off-shoot of CFM and the Marriage Encounter

Stretching the Boundaries 49

came when English-speaking and Spanish-speaking couples who had experienced the Encuentro (Encounter) met to discuss the needs of Spanish-speaking persons in CFM. Through the dialogue fostered by Gustavo and Isabel Erviti and Rafael and Berta Davilla, a separate section of CFM was established, the Movimiento Familiar Christiano. Encouraged by Bishop Patricio Flores to concentrate on the tremendous potential of the family to transform society and to help family members lead more human, meaningful lives, the MFC now encompasses people of twenty different nationalities in their own organization.

Boundaries were stretching in every direction. A young student from Nigeria, Eddie Taiso, heard about CFM while a visitor in a CFM home in Chicago. Noting the Observe-Judge-Act model helped couples broaden their Christian vision, he and his American bride, Bessie, returned to Nigeria determined to spread the story of CFM. Encouraged by their bishop, they began the tiring rounds of visits to families, explanations of the movement and appeals to married friends. Couples did come, and later Bessie Taiwo noted: "The CFM shows us married people how to love and live at home, how to love and help our neighbors. It has made our family the happiest one on earth."

Father Pedro Richards, an anthropologist, wrote from Jalapa, Guatemala: "We had tried everything to change the centuries-old ways of the Indian home where the woman is practically a slave. Now that we have a few hundred Indian families in CFM, the husband has not only stopped beating his wife, but he lets her talk and even listens to her advice."

From Kamakura City in Japan, a CFM husband wrote: "We in Japan hardly had meetings outside of the home where husband and wife sat together. This system of CFM is entirely new to us. The fact that we now get together to discuss and act is our most noteworthy accomplishment. Now our wives walk alongside us, instead of behind us husbands, which surprises many people."

In Ghana, traditions were broken as families decided to take their meals in common, as husband and wife went out and participated in activities together. "Husbands must help their wives in some household duties, without consideration for human respect," they reported. "We discussed the problem of the dowry and reached the conclusion that the dowry (money or goods needed by the wife to take with her into marriage) is necessary and unavoidable. However, everyone must strive for the lowering of the rate and the abolition of the bargaining it entails."

Pat and Patty Crowley circled the globe several times, tracking down every person who wrote to the CFM National Office for material. As they networked contacts, national federations sprouted in New Zealand, Canada, the Philippines, Majorca, Japan, Ghana, India and Australia.

In Latin America, the Movimiento Familiar Christiano connected family groups in Brazil, Argentina, Mexico, Uruguay, Bolivia and Chile. In 1963, CFMers from the United States were invited to the MFC Assembly in Rio de Janeiro. They listened as speakers Dom Helder Camara and Chaplain Lucas Moreira Never spoke about action to bring about the "entire restoration, humane and Christian, of the unprotected people and form new families which will be happier in a better world."

The eight hundred couples in attendance, who had traveled at their own expense from Mexico, Argentina, Chile, Puerto Rico, Costa Rica, Uruguay, Bolivia, Peru, Venezuela, El Salvador, Ecuador, Honduras, Guatemala, Santa Domingo, Colombia, Nicaragua, the United States and Canada listened to the tremendous challenge to "extend their hands to the serious problems in social, political, moral, economic and educational sectors which weigh heavily on our families." Change would not come easily.

In 1966, Steve Landregan of the *Texas Catholic*, his wife, Virginia, and other North American CFMers traveled to the MFC Assembly in Caracas. Again came the call, given by Pepe and Luzma Alvarez-Icaza of Mexico, the only couple to be invited to attend Vatican II, asking the delegates to "stop being so self-centered that we shut out all problems so as not to suffer from them." The Alvarez-Icazas went on to say: "We have to reform our attitudes regarding situations considered dangerous, contaminating. Let us all become contaminated. Let us all have the Christian boldness to stretch out our hand to the divorcees, social outcasts, so as to bring Christian love to them all."

Yet, the Landregans went on to say, "CFM is *the* movement in Latin America and while only ten years old it has already worked minor miracles. It has had two principal effects. It has created a great new social consciousness among the growing middle class; it has integrated the family into a single unit, particularly with regard to the role of wives. The spirit and zeal, the hundreds of small meetings in which couples, priests, sisters and bishops sat down to discuss the problems facing their nations and developing workable solutions were inspiring and an indication of the determination with which the Church in Latin America is implementing Vatican II."

In 1964 in the ACT issue, "*Christianity or Chaos*," editor Tim Murnane reported on the first meeting of CICOP, the Catholic Inter-American Cooperation Program. There was another call to CFMers as Monsignor Joseph Gremillion insisted, "Nothing less than society-wide revolution, a non-violent, democratic revolution but nonetheless a folding up of the old order and the unfolding of a new system of human relations comes to pass." And Father Vincent Lovett of the *Catholic Reporter* in Kansas City warned: "Much more important than what a priest says is what he does and what he is. There can be no effective bond of unity between North and South America if we maintain the divorce of theology from crude reality, religion from life and spirituality from its mission and responsibility."

The Editorial Committee of *ACT* — Don Thorman, Michael Greene, Dan O'Connell, Bernard Daly, Barbara Sylvain, Tom Kennedy, Earl Fischer and Marianne Nelson —

narrowed the focus of responsibility to CFMers as families were fed the message of Pope John XXIII's encyclical "Peace on Earth," of Cardinal Meyer's Lenten message: "It is not enough to see, we must begin to act...more than giving up of candy or cigarettes." Barb and Jerry Ryan of Pittsburgh wrote of the possibility that "primary poverty can be wiped out — for the first time in history."

The emphasis during 1965 on Observe-Judge-Act placed heavy responsibility on the increasing number of CFMers as they moved beyond their own neighborhoods and communities and saw injustice. They were called to move beyond national boundaries to identify with the tragedies taking place in the world community. Not all couples were happy with this emphasis.

International Confederation of Christian Family Movements

Yet in 1966 the Christian Family Movement made a giant leap forward in Caracas as the Movimiento Familiar Christiano and the CFM representatives agreed to form a new organization, The International Confederation of Christian Family Movements, A United Nation of Families.

In retrospect, these Latin groups, working against tremendous odds, studying the Gospel together and acting for nonviolent social change, were, as James Hug, S.J. has suggested, the precursors of the base communities now in Latin America. At the ICCFM meeting which was held in 1974 in Tanzania, in conjunction with families from the World Council of Churches, members of the CFM saw another picture of injustice and poverty. Paolo Friere, exiled educator from Brazil, led couples through tumultuous waters as members from 51 countries, of every race, color and economic level, struggled to find a common bond between the two worlds of privilege and poverty.

A different time and place from the meeting in Caracas, the couples saw, in the Ujamma villages of Tanzania, where they worked, a people laboring, as Nelly de

Aniano of Uruguay said, "not because it is an obligation, but because their work is *history* and they are aware of this." A new solidarity was forged as participants lived in primitive conditions, deeply affected by being part of a struggle of a new country forging its destiny. Stately Sarah Nyirenda of Tanzania, born under colonialism, aging gracefully under her own flag, told us, "We are not here to place blame for existing patterns, but here we are, we must start with the church, for we are all members of the church. We must destroy the Christian myths that relegate women to a second-place position. We must start with politicians who find it easy to talk about the liberation of women — we must force them to put into practice in their own lives and homes what they articulate in public."

In FAMILIA '74, as the meeting was called, convictions and beliefs were deepened, broken, rebuilt, changed, discovered as the forty small groups of eight to fifteen people traveled over dirt roads, in old buses, to work with primitive tools in cooperative fields belonging to the people. New facts bombarded our consciousness: when Tanzania became an independent nation there were only five persons who held a Master's Degree. In Uruguay young husbands were making the life-changing decision to retreat to the hills. From South Africa, a Methodist minister and father was asked, "Why did you come? Won't you be in trouble when you return home?" And the reply, "I came because my sons are saying to me, 'Why have you stood for this apartheid so long? Isn't it better to die like a man than live like a dog?'" Our friend told us he was risking going to prison because he had participated in an integrated meeting.

Paolo Friere summed it up for us: "An educational experience such as this in the heart of the Tanzania experience, together with sufficient time for people to reflect on that experience, as well as their own reactions, offers opportunities for everyone to discover new levels of critical awareness about themselves, their society and the world." Life could never be the same.

The work of the formation of conscience continued in the yearly program books, while *ACT* articles exposed the dehumanizing effect of racism and exploitation on every continent. Rays of hope also appeared as Dr. Al Fonder, a CFMer who had worked in Peru, told the story of Maryknoller Dan McClellan whose people, in the high Andes, were desperately poor — thirty-five thousand people living in earth-floored mud huts. Starting with an investment of twenty-four American dollars, the Puno people with Padre Dan's help started a credit union which eventually blossomed into an organization of 250 credit unions. "There is suffering, unbelievable suffering in the barrios of Rio, the mountains of Peru," said Al. "But where people have answered the call to unite themselves to the suffering in Latin America there is hope of a resurrection, even in the worldly sense."

On another front, the ICCFM and International Center of Family Studies organized a world assembly in Rome to respond to Pope John Paul's Synod, *The Role of the Family in the Modern World*. Comments came from the Tomontos and Hamiltons of the United States and Roly and Isabelle Leroux of Canada, President-couple of the ICCFM:

> We were overjoyed to read in the documents that the family is reiterated as the domestic church within the larger community, sharing the pastoral work of evangelization, family ministry, charged with fostering social justice.
>
> However, we were disturbed to see entrenched phrases such as, "frailty," "human weakness," "unequal to the task," used to describe some Christian couples' response. We know too many persons who are struggling with themselves and their consciences.
>
> What is an international, ecumenical, but primarily Catholic organization like ICCFM to do with our couples in Japan where mixed marriages are increasing? What do we say to our couples in Thailand when a Muslim marries a Catholic? We cannot send them to the Office for Christian Unity for solutions to marital problems. We must fit our faith

into family situations. We want to see a tone that would say, "Look, we may not always agree, but it doesn't mean we don't always love."

The participants in the World Assembly also heard the challenge, given in the words of Father Bill Dyson from Canada's Vanier Institute who spoke of simplicity in lifestyle for families, how materialism brings spiritual poverty, and the role of ICCFM for change.

CFM National Convention at Notre Dame

The church was being called to a theology in which people mattered as boundaries became meaningless. It was at the yearly gathering of CFMers at the National Convention at the University of Notre Dame that the theology would be hammered out. Theologians, professionals, the "people in the pews," would listen to each other, grapple with issues, strive for understanding and the ability to "live for 24 hours in another person's shoes," as Jesuit John L. Thomas would say. Respect for each person's experience and competence gave courage to continue looking for a way out of the modern maze in which we were trapped.

The siege of the Notre Dame campus by Christian Family Movement people began in the '50s. In 1952, Father Ted Hesburgh, the newly appointed president of the university, spoke to the CFMers: "If we get canonized couples in this country, as I think we will, it will probably come as a result of this movement — with which I've been familiar since 1945 when it was just an idea in the heads of a few people." His support and friendship never faltered as the small group, a trickle of a hundred families, grew into hundreds of families and then thousands. By plane, car, station wagon, bus and camper, families invaded the campus, this glorious mecca.

For the first time women and children invaded the student halls. Onto the campus, into the hallowed halls, poured mothers, fathers, children of every age, priests, bishops, sisters. For three decades they came to the CFM convention at Notre Dame to be energized by the vision of the future.

In the early days families were housed in the old dormitories, Farley Hall and Dillon Hall, sleeping in the ancient, high, double-decker iron beds — a novelty to be mastered which came, jokingly, to be called "the new birth control method" by the couples. The double-deckers posed other hazards. Father Louis Putz approached a young woman during morning Mass, whispering, "Is this yours?" The startled mother glanced down to see a very rumpled two-year-old in his pajamas clasping Father Putz's hand. Left in his father's care, Billy had crawled out of the lower bunk, walked the long corridors, through the swinging doors of the chapel, while Daddy slept soundly in the upper bunk.

The hospitality of the South Bend CFM groups was legend. While Ralph and Reggie Weissert and their CFM group hunted up baby cribs, mattresses and ran errands for the hard-working convention committee, others were preparing for a real honest-to-goodness folk dancing party at Helene and Bernie Bauer's barn.

A corps of exceptional teenagers took over the task of baby-sitting, which became a school for good fun. Divided into age groups, kids went on field trips, sang songs, learned to dance. Hundreds of babies were fed, diapered, and persuaded to nap; and when day was done, the teenagers gathered in the famous Huddle to swap stories. Year after year young friends would regroup to continue building a store of memories and friendships.

Not all was sweetness and light for the hosting university, unused to a roaming horde of, sometimes, a thousand youngsters, ranging in age from two months to seventeen years. It was hard not to fantasize about the possibility for disaster or anarchy. Not enough credit can be given to the remarkable teenagers who worked, smiling, cajoling, loving, tenderly shepherding their charges. Surprise was always just around the corner. There was the year twelve-year-old John wanted to "see what would happen" if he pulled the fire alarm in one of the dorms. He did, and all hell broke loose: the University fire department and the South Bend fire crew raced to the scene, only to discover it was a false alarm. Neither the firefighters, the university administration, nor the parents were amused, but the story remains a "Remember when...."

Fortunate were CFMers who made the trek to Notre Dame, the CFM "University of the People." With their compatriots they stood in the long lines in the cafeteria, shared the fun of being together at the evening parties, swapped stories of the successes and failures of their actions and exchanged addresses for further meetings.

There was an embarrassment of riches as the couples were overwhelmed by the cache of jewels presented in the speakers and workshops. In 1965, five thousand people attended the 15th Convention. Delegates came from thirty-eight countries, and with the sixteen hundred couples there were a thousand children. Special sessions covered the topics of Inner-City Diocesan Programs, The Role of Women, Mission Vacations, The Outgrowth of the Program on Race and Politics, Rural CFM, and The Theology of Married Love (conducted by Father Bernard Haring).

Seminars dealt with Christian Family Prayer; The Mass of the Future; Insight into Latin America, Southeast Asia, Africa; The History of the Teaching on Contraception in the Catholic Church; Changing Cultural Patterns in the World; A New Look at Peace; and An Appreciation of the Arts.

Speakers included Martin and Katherine Quigley, Father Louis Putz, Professor John Noonan, Mary Perkins Ryan, Monsignor Luigi Ligutti, Genevieve Caulfield, Elizabeth Reid, Father Francois Houtart and Frank Getlein.

Not to be ignored, young Maureen Fitzgerald of New York instigated a program of workshops especially for teenagers.

Gathering in the massive Stepan Center, that frolic of imagination which resulted in the design of the silver-colored futuristic geodesic dome which shimmered in the sunlight, we were enchanted by the arrangement. The dome looked like a gigantic silver pouf worn by the ladies of the eighteenth century. Father Paul Valente was to rise during the gathering to "thank the thousands of Notre Dame students who had saved the silver paper in Hershey bars for years in order to provide the silver coverings for Stepan Center." The design was a sign of the future and we reveled in the opportunity to share in the future church by bringing Vatican II into reality.

The prophets were among us: Jesuit Gustav Weigel, George Schuster, Dr. Martin Marty, John Tracy Ellis, Tom Dooley, Carl Stokes, Paul Simon, Father John MacKenzie, Dan Berrigan, Henri Nouwen, Gregory Baum, Dr. Joseph Ford, Dr. Joseph Sittler, Monsignor Pietro Pavan, Joe and Madelyn Bonsignore, Matt Ahmann, Joseph Lichten, Dan and Donna Fitzpatrick, Father John Curnow of New Zealand, Bishop Charles Buswell, Jesuit Louis Twomey, Pepe and Luzma Alvarez-Icaza, Father Ted Syrianey. And, always, in the background, Monsignor Reynold Hillenbrand, who would not let us rest as he pushed us further into the forest of foment to confront the dragons. And — Pat and Patty Crowley. Patty to mother each person at the Convention, keep things organized, the foil for all of Pat's jokes; and Pat, full of wisdom, pretending he was not a great thinker; both of them mentors for the thousands of couples who came to celebrate their involvement in CFM. And, with Pat and Patty, their own children, Patsy, Cathy, Pat, Theresa, and all the other "children" who happened to be living with them at the time.

In the heady atmosphere of the silver-coated Stepan Center, we were enclosed in a womb of joy. Brilliant banners brought by CFM groups from across the country encircled the great hivelike auditorium. Clusters of men and women, deep in discussion, made a sound like a million bees buzzing.

One wonderfully memorable year, Father Clarence

Rivers gathered 3500 people milling under the silver pouf into a magnificent choir. Coaxing, cajoling, this talented young priest-musician pressed us to sing the Mass he had composed. Thirty-five hundred voices gathered momentum as the sound wove its way in and around the people until it seemed one voice rising into the great silver ceiling. That day, for the first time at a CFM Convention, a *woman* rose to read the Epistle. We knew we had entered a new time.

The documents of Vatican II validated the work and the vision of CFM, whose valiant program committees had led us to study and anticipate the Council's call for the vernacular in the Liturgy, the empowerment of the people. There was more unexplored territory and the program committee forged ahead. Books dealt with Shalom: Peace in the Family, in the City, in the World; Understanding and Building Community; Revaluing Christian Commitment; Work, Money and Your Family; Discovering Christ; The Quality of Life; Discovering Others; Ministering Together; Come Through Life with Me. Meetings were not simple: Human Rights and the Elderly; The Funeral in Your Future; Social Justice and Minority Business; The Call to Witness; Liberty and Justice — For All?; Pills, Pot and Booze; What Price Success?; Ministering to Families; Women and the New Feminism; Swords into Plowshares; The Sweat of Whose Brow?; Leisure: A Time for Recreating; Hungry People; Violence; The Earth and its Resources; Justice and Love. There would be no slowing down the call of Scripture to go out and see the world, ask if people are cared for and risk involvement through action.

Boundaries were stretched beyond the small horizon some CFMers believed was the real horizon. Families, husbands and wives, teenagers and little children stretched and stretched and then stretched again. Beyond the small horizon they would find themselves, as Teilhard said, "united with all those who, from every direction, have made the same ascent."

CHAPTER VI
The Turbulent Years

The Family in a Time of Revolution
People born too late to live the life for
which they were conditioned. And too
early to live the life they envision.
CFM Inquiry Program, 1970

The 1970 inquiry brought into focus the plight of families of the sixties and seventies, buffetted by movements outside their control. The sparks which had been smoldering in church and society burst into fires, kindled by demands for change. Crucial questions raised by the civil rights movement, the sexual revolution and the Vietnam War fanned the flames. No family remained untouched; CFMers were not immune.

Couples were reminded of the complexity of life in the introduction to the 1970 program. "Things like protest and militancy, racism, busing, housing and restless students are all around us. There are quieter and personal revolutions, too - what is happening to old people, to the family and its money, how men and women express their feelings in and out of marriage."

Early on, Jesuit Joe Fichter, sociologist and teacher, reminded CFMers at a National Convention at Notre Dame:

Reform, progress, experimentation, adaptation have become contemporary American values. Some Catholics are afraid of change, some resist because it threatens hallowed traditions, because it requires a new kind of alertness and vigilance, because it makes demands. There is no room for a tradition-bound apostle in modern America. A group is not apostolic if it is thinking more of preservation than of reformation.

Civil Rights

Already in the 1956 program, Inquiries dealt with prejudice — an unnerving experience for couples untouched by the disease and its effects. Titled *Social Harmony*, the book encouraged couples to seriously make observations, take a look at the findings in light of the Gospel and act. For the couples who courageously went out to gather information in their communities, the viciousness of racial discrimination was shattering. They had read a report from the Illinois Institute of Technology which said in part: "Wide differences exist in the difficulty of placing individuals of various ethnic groups even when all are equally qualified ... Irish, English and German applicants are easy to place, whereas only two percent of Negroes, Mexicans and Orientals are easy to place." Getting the information firsthand by actually going out and talking to people exposed the chasm. Groups took small, tentative steps to cross the bridge which separated races, threading their way through unknown territory.

In Dubuque, Iowa, CFMers asked the City Council for a report on segregation in the city. In Portland, Oregon, couples approached Governor Holmes to enlist his support for a law making it illegal for Realtors to discriminate against minorities. The tentative steps grew into longer and longer strides.

In Clinton, Iowa, CFMers Don and Joan Randall and Vern and Maureen Witt worked with church groups and community leaders to sponsor an Interfaith Symposium on Religion and Race. Reporting on the meeting at the Sacred Heart Church Hall with 450 people present, the *Clinton Herald* noted: "The community of Clinton accomplished something on Sunday night never before done in the

The Turbulent Years

108-year-old history of this city. For the first time Negro, White, Protestant and Catholic clergy and laypeople sat down together for an honest, organized, civilized meeting of minds." Out of the meeting came fourteen study groups using the CFM Inquiry method. A Commission on Human Relations was established, high school "town meetings" on interracial and interdenominational topics were held, sixteen college students surveyed the city to determine its racial profile and many industries and merchants quietly dropped hidden racial barriers.

In Syracuse, New York, couples formed an interfaith, interracial community "peace corps," linking suburbia and the inner city. In Lewiston, New York, after an exchange of home visits and listening to speakers, couples felt they were not really getting to know each other. A party was the answer. Reinforced by ham sandwiches and a keg of beer, the couples talked about the things they all thought and worried about: kids, schools, jobs, politics.

In Canada the CFMers used the race meetings to analyze the situation of Indians. In Saskatoon a bicultural dialogue with the French was begun. In Delhi, Ontario, inquiries focused on Eskimo relations.

In Tennessee, Bill and Laura Caldwell were targeted as "nigger lovers" as they helped integrate the city swimming pool. Later Laura was to write: "People are anxious to talk about the terrible conditions in the South, but not to confront the problems in their own Northern communities."

Not all CFMers and the clergy were pleased at the continued emphasis on race in Social Inquiries and in the CFM magazine, *ACT*. Defensive and angry letters, with resignations from membership, repose now in peace in the archives of Notre Dame, indicating the depth of the resentment and condemnation of the program book.

But Hilly gave us no respite. In the face of criticism that the program committee was "going too far away from family life," he would say,

> Formative work is going on whether we appreciate or not the way it (the Inquiry) opens up new fields for us. An apostle must want to think as our Lord thinks on all the problems of life ... It is fine to help a neighbor when there is a new baby, but we must do more than that ... A person can be a person of exquisite individual charity and still not be formed. Suppose I was good to my neighbor, helped on my block and at the parish, but had the wrong thinking about Negroes and Jews ... Suppose I wouldn't want Negroes in my neighborhood, or my children to play with their children and would welcome anti-Semitic jokes. Then, I say, such a person, for all his charity and being in CFM, is a scandal to the church and to CFM. We are either building up Christ's body or tearing it apart.

These were heavy words for couples educated in church, school and society, without the question of the immorality of prejudice ever being raised.

By 1964, the Inquiry book *Race and Politics* was unequivocal in its emphasis on serious participation by the couples in the area of justice for black citizens. The yearly program tackled racism head on. Titled, *Encounter with Politics and Race*, the call was clearly dramatized in the Introduction:

> The Social Inquiry program you are about to undertake is a bold call to action. The plan on which it is built is very simple and very clear. Every member must get to know persons who run for office ... must retain interest in matters of government after the excitement of elections is over. Every member of CFM must also seek out and come to know a Negro. Every Negro must seek out and come to know a white person. He must have this close personal encounter with a Negro or Negro family, so that he will finally see not a person distinguished by color but a man different only in his God-given individuality. Every member of CFM, beyond this act of friendship and love, must take an active part in the organized movement for civil rights for all.
>
> What is simple is not necessarily easy. But if CFM members should not become involved in politics or civil

The Turbulent Years

rights, they would not only deny the goals of CFM, they would deny their Christian witness.

The year 1964 proved to be a great challenge to the CFM couples in every corner of the country. The fire for justice would not be quenched, but would roar with great turmoil for all concerned.

Participation in the Selma march and civil rights demonstrations with Rev. Martin Luther King, Jr., and their black brothers and sisters, broke the hearts of many CFMers; priests, nuns, and laypeople who experienced the terror of the cancerous ulcer now exposed to the light. On the home front acrimony increased. Seeds of discord were sown as labels of "subversive," "communist" and "un-American" were bandied about. The times were a test of commitment and understanding for CFMers that theology is to be lived.

In Alexandria, Virginia, Michael Ambrose and Charles Moran, CFMers from Blessed Sacrament Parish, were sent to Montgomery, Alabama, to carry a banner proclaiming: "Virginia CFM believes: NO VOTE, NO HOPE." The men were sent, they said, to "educate our minds and emotions so we might help educate those who could not go." Their account was vivid:

> As our cab drove through a group of workers we were spat upon. We stood several hours in the mud at St. Jude's with twenty-five thousand people waiting for directions. We marched through streets lined with living malevolence to stand at the capitol, a testimony to the efficacy of a nonviolent movement. There were people in their fifties and sixties, some on crutches, all tired - no one complained. Marching through the Negro section we sang freedom songs and waved American flags - but we felt the hatred of the people in the white neighborhoods. They stared ... with open hostility and condemned us and we judged them in return, though we shouldn't have.
>
> In a way they were pitiable, these white people whom we had put on a spot. We were too many to be treated with contempt. They could spit on the first hundred rabbis, the

first thousand ministers and priests, deride the businessmen and housewives, but as the march went on ... as people who looked no less respectable than they grew to twenty-five thousand, they must have had a terrible suspicion that they were wrong - that they were protesting something as archaic as the secession their flags proclaimed and as the murder of a young man protecting his mother, or the murder of a minister following his conscience in Selma.

There were just too many people, from too many walks of life, to be treated with contempt. Near the end of the march we were honored with praise appropriate to the occasion. It was uttered as an epithet, but when a group of men called us "nigger lovers," we knew we had been recognized as people following Christ's command to love our neighbors as ourselves. A young Negro girl, thinking we might be offended, told us those men were sick. She was right and more Christ-like than any of us. One of us had asked our cabbie if he thought the march would open people's eyes and he answered, "I think it will open some people's hearts."

Returning to Alexandria, Michael and Charles told their story and the Alexandria CFMers moved into action, establishing a tutoring program for the Negro students transferring to all-white schools. Other denominations helped. Thirty-five couples were matched with individual students as the gap between the youngsters' education and experience was bridged.

The effect of CFM programs on race relations in communities called to awareness spread across a barren land. In Louisville, Knoxville, St. Louis, Chicago, interracial and interfaith home visits blossomed. In Lansing CFMers investigated discriminatory real estate advertising. In Rockford couples campaigned for freedom of residence in local cooperative housing. The couples knew that the Supreme Court decision on school integration changed only the law; it did not convert minds and hearts. Change had to take place on the neighborhood and community level and it was here that the average CFMer did the indispensable job of creating a favorable public opinion toward racial justice.

In Chicago, the massive Cabrini public housing project was home for the city's poor. In the gigantic structures, the predominantly Negro population and some Spanish-speaking families had lost contact with parishes. A census was imperative.

Monsignor John Egan of the Chicago Conservation Council turned to Jim and Helen Hassett and Chaplain Larry Kelly of the CFM Federation for assistance. In a historic effort, more than three hundred CFMers and other laypeople formed teams including volunteers, a local resident and a chaplain to canvass the monstrous structures. Twenty-seven hundred families were contacted as the laypeople of Chicago crossed neighborhood and parish boundaries, becoming intimately involved in bringing Christ to a geographically and culturally separate community.

Father Andy Greeley noted an old and legless Negro woman being evicted. "She was taken home, to be cared for by a couple, to a neighborhood where Negroes were not welcome." Moved by the suffering and injustice present in this subhuman complex, John and Helen Daly, Sal and Stephanie Ferrara and Roland and Mabel Higgs began a long-range program of involving CFMers with the people of Cabrini.

The struggle was intense and the conflict was everywhere. Fifty-year-old pastor Father John V. Coffield of Los Angeles' Ascension Catholic Church announced he would go into "self-imposed exile as the strongest protest" he could make against Cardinal James Francis McIntyre's racial policies. Coffield said he had been repeatedly reprimanded by McIntyre for his advocacy of racial and civil rights and had been ordered out of the state on a forced "vacation" once for his outspokenness. Coffield took up residence in Chicago where he worked in a Southside parish with a large Negro membership. His speaking engagements subsequently were curtailed in Chicago, also.

Two years a priest, twenty-seven-year-old Father Phillip Berryman gave his first sermon on racial injustice in Los Angeles on May 9, 1965 and two days later was transferred. His pastor, said Berryman, told him after he preached two masses that some parishioners had complained. Two days later, he was called before Cardinal James Francis McIntyre and Auxiliary Bishop Timothy Manning and informed — with no reason given — that he was being transferred to an all-white parish academy for girls where his only duties would be to say Mass and hear confessions.

At the yearly CFM Convention, Sargent Shriver declared:

> The crisis (of race) is *not* in the slums, but in the suburbs. The poor are like they are, not because of what they have done, but because of what the rich haven't done. To love, we must put ourselves in the skin of another and be weakened by those burdens. We must risk failure; to not have a concern for being a religion of success but rather a religion of love. It is a war against attitudes.

In Detroit, Jim and Betsy Carr coordinated efforts to house people coming to the Poor People's March. Working with the NAACP, Interfaith Action Council, and the Archdiocesan Human Relations Committee, 2,000 people were housed in a week. The community responded. Pastors opened their rectories in the city and suburbs, colleges opened their dorms. "We'll take a family of five, we'll take four males, I can handle two females" came the offers. The response was tremendous and was accomplished primarily through the structures and human resources of CFM.

Cathy Scalise, CFM leader from Erie, Pennsylvania, went to work for HANDS, Inc. (Housing and Neighborhood Development Service), an offshoot of a CFM group which specialized in interracial activities. HANDS was the first non-profit housing group in the area to enter into the FHA project of rehabilitation and home ownership. In support, CFMers gave monthly sustaining pledges, physical labor,

The Turbulent Years

clothing, furnishings, and just plain friendship.

In Erie, Pennsylvania, CFMers Jim Toohey, Jim Wagner, Charlie Scalise, and Father John Poux were appointed by the mayor to serve on the Model Cities advisory committee. In Syracuse, John and Pat Eitel were appointed CFM representatives to the new Inner City Board.

In Detroit, old and new CFM members were successful in moving twenty families, uprooted by summer riots, to new housing. The growing groups, some called HANDS, some HOPE, around the country were ecumenical efforts in many cities to provide housing for families in need.

In Milwaukee, Don O'Connell, with the help of his wife, Mary, won a position on the Milwaukee School Board. Don's decision to run came because he felt

> the socio-economic order in Milwaukee has to be rejuvenated, perfected. As a CFMer, although we can be very active on the fringes of politics by exerting pressure as private citizens, it is only when we actually become a member of the power structure itself can we exert our maximum Christian impact. If we want to change the situation, we have to get in there."

The issue of the campaign was de facto segregation in the public schools. Three CFM couples were litigants in a federal court alleging that de facto segregation is harmful to children. Mary agreed with Don:

> The school board's responsibility lies in several directions, including education and welfare. Since we live in a multi-racial city, children of different races must learn to live together.

Birth Control

The fires of change did not die. The question of birth control, festering in the womb of the Catholic Church, became apparent in the early sixties.

In 1964, in an attempt to deal with the question, Pope Paul VI established a Special Study Group on Population and Birth Control. Pat and Patty Crowley, President-couple of the Christian Family Movement, were one of three couples appointed to the commission, a tribute to their tireless work for families and their fidelity to the church.

Asked to find out couples' experience using the rhythm method, the Crowleys designed, with the help of the Notre Dame University's and Georgetown University's sociology departments, a questionnaire for wide distribution to married people. In *ACT*, a debate on birth control was in progress, partly in response to the article "Catholics and Contraception" by John Noonan and a set of ten questions inviting readers' comments.

A flood of mail resulted. Some correspondents insisted church teaching was wrong, others declared obedience to church authority, others expressed confusion. For every letter welcoming the discussion, there was a canceled subscription to *ACT*.

The Crowleys were inundated by letters, most of them from women who unloaded burdens they had carried for years. Most of the writers were in their early thirties and had, on the average, five children. Shaken by what they were reading, Pat and Patty sent copies of the letters to the commission secretary in the hope they would eventually reach the pope.

History records there was a remarkable change in discussion and thinking among the members of the commission as they came into contact with intimate details of the lives of faithful Christians. As the end of the work of the commission neared, two reports were prepared for the Holy Father; a majority and a minority report. The majority report favored a change in the strictures of church policy, regarding birth control as not intrinsically evil, and that the doctrine of *Casti Conubi* could be changed. The commission disbanded, members returned to their countries; the Crowleys and others presumed the majority report would be honored. The year was 1966.

While Rome pondered the issue, 1966 and 1967

passed. Meanwhile, statistics indicated American Catholics had decided for themselves to accept the Pill. Yet no word came from the Vatican. In July 1968, the encyclical *Humanae Vitae* was issued, rejecting the advice the majority of the commission had given Pope Paul VI. It was a serious blow to the members of the commission who had worked selflessly to discern the needs of conscientious couples.

Within a week the Crowleys joined with John Noonan, Andre Hellegers and two hundred scholars to take exception to the encyclical. The public dissent of the Crowleys cost them the support of Chicago's highest ranking prelate and the friendship of the man who had been their inspiration for twenty-five years. "Cardinal Cody has never talked to us (after the dissent) and neither has Monsignor Hillenbrand," Patty reported several years later.

To Patty, *Humanae Vitae* was a sudden, unprovoked blow. Pat felt the discussion of the issue should continue but people were no longer interested. In the fall of 1968, response to another survey of couples in the International CFM was only a trickle. While Pat disagreed with the pope's directive, he could not understand why anyone would leave the church because of it. "Their faith couldn't have amounted to much," he would say on one occasion; and besides, "there are *other* issues facing the world and the church."

In the whirlwind of the sexual revolution, the biweekly meetings of CFM provided a safe haven. Husbands and wives could struggle with the questions of sexuality, pornography, birth responsibility and abortion in a community of support. Ill-prepared for living in a time of revolution, they hung together, planning seminars on sexuality and workshops on family communication in parishes and schools. In Portland, Maine, CFM and the Confraternity of Christian Doctrine joined forces to sponsor an Institute on Sex Education for parents and teenagers, drawing twelve hundred participants.

Economic Justice

Through the birth control controversy, the "other issues" in the church called for attention. Two great encyclicals of Pope John XXIII brought church and society face to face with the social dilemmas of the times. Studying *Mater et Magistra (Christianity and Social Progress)*, CFM couples faced questions of job and income security, government and the economy, personal property, international justice, the dignity of work, and economic pressures on the family. Minds stretched as couples struggled to comprehend the implications of basic injustices in the economic system, a topic the American bishops were to pursue much later.

Massive remedies were required in the economic arena. The CFMers started at home base working for just labor conditions, finding jobs, working to end discrimination in hiring and engaging in union activity. Researching earlier church involvement in the cooperative movement, CFMers acted to form parish credit unions. In an East Los Angeles parish school, youngsters learned the principles of cooperation by forming their own credit union and administering its funds.

Returning from the ICCFM meeting held in New Zealand in 1971, Dan and I reported in *ACT*:

> "Revolution begins at our place," said buttons worn at the New Zealand National Convention. There is little doubt the demand for radical change is the unifying call of young and old. That is the impression that overwhelmed us. Though the crises in the United States are great, they are mirrored in varying degrees in every country we visited: Australia, Philippines, Tahiti, Fiji, Hawaii.
>
> Yes, we can assure you, a Third World does indeed exist. It is a world with which each of us must deal, soon. This is the world where education is for the few, where hunger stalks hourly, where conspicuous consumption stands next to destitution, where sub-human poverty is a fact of life, and where a rising chorus of voices is demanding to know why

six percent of the world's population controls sixty percent of the world's goods.

Most of the adults agreed that "change must and will come, but it will take time." The young, however, said in effect: "On the surface things are fine, but we know that minority groups in our country do not have the same rights we do. We are not going to stand around and let this continue."

To the young the global village is a reality. Instant communication has dramatized the fact of discrimination and injustice throughout the world. In Tahiti we were told: "The French are in control, but this is our land and we will have it back." In Australia, we heard, "The Aborigines have been kept in the hills deliberately." In Hawaii, a young university student told us, "I am going to be a history teacher and I will teach the history of *my* people, not the history of the white man."

At the ICCFM, the Philippine CFMers reported of a manifesto they issued to the entire country: "*We Can No Longer Sit and Watch and Wait*, aligning the movement with "youth in their legitimate demands to correct the social, economic and religious ills of our country." The CFMers joined their compatriots in calling for a new Constitutional Convention for their country. (It would be sixteen years before the new Constitution would be adopted. In the meantime, members of CFM families would be imprisoned with other citizens.)

From Latin America came news of CFM groups organizing father-son meetings to deal with the imminent upheavals in society. Their sense of urgency was stark: "Either there will be immediate, peaceful, revolutionary changes in Latin America or there will soon be dreaded revolutions."

We left home believing the turmoil in our country was peculiar to our time and place. We know it is not; revolution is a fact. Whether it is peaceful depends to a great extent on our ability to face the grim realities in our world.

The putrid pollution we saw is indescribable. We felt the bitterness of people because "American businesses discriminate against us in the good positions" and "control of our economy is not in our hands."

For 21 days of travel we lived with families, talking to parents, students, professionals, servants, workers. When people believed we honestly wanted to learn, we were taken outside the "tourist circle." The picture is not pretty: naked children living in tin shacks without water or sanitation, playing in running sewage in the streets, grown-ups old and tired cutting sugar by hand in the near dark. We saw steaming groups of teenagers hanging around corners; told 1,000 youths a day enter the job market. Not far away were beatiful homes surrounded by concrete walls, topped with jagged glass, surmounted by three rounds of barbed wire. Streets were protected by police at the gated entrances to the Catholic college built to educate the children of the rich.

When we asked if any poor youngsters attend the college, we were told this "poses a problem, but it is hard. If the poor students come to the college, they will see how little they have in comparison to the other students. And, if they come in buses, they will see the homes of the wealthy, this might cause dissatisfaction. Some of the religious would like to have some of the poor students come to the school."

We also saw priests and nuns living with the poor, holding University classes, teaching men, women, and children to build their own cooperative centers for production.

In all of this we have hope. It is because of the young who believe the Gospel is to be lived that people can make a change and discover a sense of solidarity with the whole family of God.

Peace

By the time the encyclical *Pacem in Terris (Peace on Earth)* appeared, every CFMer knew life would never be the same. Compassionately and insistently, "good Pope John" outlined the challenges facing the world family. Human rights, freedom to follow conscience, the right to emigrate and immigrate, political rights, began the litany. The reciprocity of rights and duties between persons, responsibility for a social life in truth, justice, charity and freedom, solidarity, the proper balance between population, land and capital, refugees, continued the roll-call.

Pope John XXIII, lover of people, genius of the 20th century, spoke prophetically: "Peace on earth, which men of every era have most eagerly yearned for, can be firmly established only if the order laid down by God be dutifully observed." Again, "Justice, right reason and humanity urgently demand that the arms race should cease; that the stockpiles which exist in various countries should be reduced equally and simultaneously by the parties concerned; that nuclear weapons should be banned; that a general agreement should eventually be reached about progressive disarmament and effective method of control." With exquisite insight, John had articulated the yearning of humanity for a world of justice and peace. *Pacem in Terris* brought the fundamental issue of the evil of war and nuclear arms to the forefront of responsible thought.

The exhortations of this good and gentle man fell on fertile ground. Monsignor Hillenbrand taught us well. Action based on knowledge of Scripture, Liturgy, the doctrine of the Mystical Body and the social teachings of the church was the model for development. He had led CFM through a desert of social ignorance to a land of social awareness, calling for the development of each person's unique gift for the good of all people.

In the diocese of Los Angeles, the CFM Federation sponsored a *Pacem in Terris* Conference, one of the first in the country. In Camden and Milwaukee CFMers gathered people of many races and faiths, meeting for the International Day for Peace.

At a CFM Convention at Notre Dame, my husband Dan and I held a workshop, "Why Not a National Peace Academy?" We noted there were nine war colleges in the United States, many memorials to war heroes, but the nation had no national symbol to the serious work of building a world beyond war. Said Dan, "Some day we may be faced with peace — who will work it out? The generals, the men trained in war? Even when the president visits other countries on a peace mission he takes along military aides." Pointing out that since 1802, when West Point was founded, the U.S. had spent millions for the study of war, we asked, "Why not commit the same resources and dedication to the cause of peace?"

The enthusiastic response of the CFM Convention members provided the fuel for a campaign for a National Peace Academy. In 150 congressional districts CFMers birthed a grassroots movement supporting a national commitment to the study of peace. Holy Cross Father John Reedy and Jim Andrews of *Ave Maria* gave the concept national coverage. Notre Dame President Ted Hesburgh became an immediate and faithful supporter of the idea, and the members of CFM sent a telegram to President Lyndon Johnson asking for the establishment of a Peace Academy.

For ten years, through a one page mimeographed newsletter, *Committee for a National Peace Academy*, CFMers were appraised of progress. In the July 1, 1969, issue Dan and I reported: "In May we were invited by Congressman Halpern, and Senators Vance Hartke and Mark Hatfield to a meeting in Washington to discuss the possibility of establishing an Advisory Council for the Peace Act. At the meeting were interested representatives from forty-five organizations in the country."

Reggie and Ralph Weissert of South Bend, Indiana, spearheaded a campaign to enlist the support of their senator, Vance Hartke, asking him to co-sponsor a bill in the Senate for a National Peace Academy. In 1975, Senator Hartke and Senator Hatfield introduced a bill to "establish an educational institution in the United States" to promote understanding of "the process and state of peace and to consider the dimensions of peaceful resolution of differences." It was one of many bills presented over a period of years, none of which came to a vote. Undaunted, the CFM network kept the vision alive and growing, constantly reaching out for new support. In 1975, responding to nation-wide interest, the National Peace Academy Campaign was founded in Washington, D.C. In 1983 the bishops of the United States called for support of legislation for a National Peace Academy.

In the pastoral letter, *The Challenge of Peace*, of May 3, 1983, Section III, The Promotion of Peace, Proposals and Policies, the bishops wrote:

> In 1981, the Commission on Proposals for the National Academy of Peace and Conflict Resolution recommended the establishment of the U.S. Academy of Peace, a recommendation nearly as old as this country's constitution ... We endorse the commission's recommendation and urge all citizen's to support training in conflict resolution, non-violent resistance, and programs devoted to service to peace and education for peace ... We, too, must be prepared to do our part. We encourage churches, and educational institutions, from primary schools to colleges and institutes of higher learning, to undertake similar programs at their own initiative.

In October 1984, legislation establishing the U.S. Institute of Peace was signed into law. Ironically, it came as an amendment to the Defense Authorization Bill, twenty-one years after Pope John's call for an end to war. A CFM editorial, "The New Moment," celebrated this event.

> In an historic move, Congress passed legislation calling for the establishment of the United States Institute of Peace, on October 19, 1984.
>
> Since the year 1793, when Dr. Benjamin Rush, a surgeon and signer of the Declaration of Independence, and the freed slave and master mathematician, Benjamin Banneker, introduced a proposal for a U.S. Peace Office in the federal government, the idea has refused to go away.
>
> Little attention to this and other proposals for a peace department was given in the congressional complex. In the

later years of 1945 to 1968, ninety bills were introduced calling for some form of Peace Department. They were all aborted.

The seed cast into the wind in 1793 would not die. In 1968, at the Christian Family Movement Convention at the University of Notre Dame, Dan and Rose Lucey, who knew not of this previous activity for a Peace Academy, led a workshop "Why Not a National Peace Academy?" Enthusiastic commitment came from CFMers who returned to home base and organized support for a National Peace Academy in 150 congressional districts. Holy Cross Father John Reedy and Jim Andrews of Ave Maria Magazine propagated the idea nationally. Notre Dame President, Ted Hesburgh, became an immediate and faithful advocate.

Though sixteen years would pass before Congress would act, the vision continued. National concern of Catholics for positive action for peace was reflected in Section II of the American Bishops Pastoral on War and Peace where they recommended support for the establishment of a National Peace Academy.

In 1976 the National Peace Academy Campaign in Washington D.C. was established to urge Congress to take action. National associations and organizations, which criss-crossed a panorama of interests, called for a national center for peace education, research, training and information.

Legislation in 1981 and in 1983 introduced by Senator Spark Matsunaga and Congressman Dan Glickman for a National Peace Academy failed. While 57 Senators and 177 Representatives co-sponsored the bills, they were never brought up to a vote. It appeared the vast support of people for a symbol of national commitment to peace education and research would be thwarted.

Realizing a vote on legislation for a National Peace Academy was not possible, it was given to Senator Mark Hatfield to play the inspired role in 1984. Attaching an amendment to the Defense Authorization bill for the establishment of a peace academy, he took a giant step, forcing a vote on the will of the people for a national center to seek a different road to peace.

The vision is a reality; a tribute to the unswerving commitment of citizens who believe there can be peace through justice. The newly named U.S. Institute for Peace, is by and for the people. The seed is planted. Broad people participation is vital to the fleshing out of this first national center for the research, education and training in peace and conflict management, validating the work for peace which has been part of our national life since 1793.

The Institute will be a pulsating center for people committed to research, development, training and education. A small David, believing there is strength through peace, confronts the Goliath, believing in the power of war. Each has a role to play.

The National Peace Academy Campaign, with the people, have birthed a vision, in a new moment in history for world-good.

The long, dedicated commitment of the Christian Family Movement to the establishment of a peace academy is a great tribute to each member. Dan Lucey, peacemaker and tireless advocate for the Peace Institute, did not live to celebrate the victory.

The Vietnam War

The CFM community grew from adolescence into maturity as the flames of the Vietnam War cast a grim shadow on their lives. Campuses of the nation exploded with protests of students, young people challenged family values, adults took to the streets to force an end to the dread war. Loving CFM families provided a haven for young nomads as parents called across state boundaries asking help for their children. There was heartbreak in rebellion, but many CFM parents knew long hair and grubby jeans mirrored a sickness in society. What action could CFM families, who had learned to live with the injunction Observe-Judge-Act, take to stop an obscene war?

In Detroit, CFMers joined a nationwide boycott of all nonessential consumer goods "until the war is ended." They said, "We believe in a democracy. The people must take upon themselves the final authority and responsibility for the actions of their government."

Sister Elizabeth McAllister at the National Convention had warned, "The war is coming home and more and more people will have to go to jail.... We need small communities to build the values that will change the world.... The work before us is the spiritual dismantling of the values that keep the war going ... Change that is real is going to cost us very much."

Not all CFMers were pleased with the programs emphasizing social justice issues. In response to articles in *ACT* describing the frightful condition of the poor in Latin America, the cities of America, the India of Mother Teresa and calling families to greater commitment, angry letters arrived and membership cancellations increased. Later, the criticism would be made that the leaders of CFM were too far out in front of the people. Yet, remembering the words of Archbishop Angelo Fernandez of New Delhi, who had lived with some CFMers on his way home from the Council, "It is important to go slowly enough not to frighten those not yet on the way, yet to go fast enough not to frustrate those who are already on the way," the program committee valiantly juggled demands.

Father John L. McKenzie, SJ, had warned:

> "There will be a crisis of authority (in the church) as long as the gap exists between the leaders and the led. We lack a free, constant flow between those on the governing level and the governed. Until it is possible to approach the level of friendship rather than mere administration in the diocese or parish structure, church authority is in trouble. All members of the church must show some concern and do what they can.

In the time of turmoil, Henri Nouwen spoke to the hearts of parents at the CFM Convention in 1971. Henri told the story of a young man he knew, "Peter," later to be included in the book *The Wounded Healer*. With compassion Father Nouwen described the painful alienation of the young man who found himself a stranger in an alien land. Parents gathered after the talk to share with Henri, "You're talking about my son."

Commitment to the ideals enunciated in CFM called for giving of oneself. In facing the demands to work for peace and justice, men and women entered politics, left comfortable jobs to work with the poor. Listening to the words of the Gospel, they marched to a different drummer. Their constant study and action laid the foundation of support for the work of the bishops of the United States in the Pastoral Letter on War and Peace and the Pastoral Letter on Economics. The documents of Vatican II had validated the role of laypeople, but CFMers had learned very early that their challenge was to live out a people's theology.

CHAPTER VII
The Genius of CFM

> "The universe revolves in a milieu of order. I attempt to attain this by remembering growing up in the Christian Family Movement, having experiences which helped me to develop order in my adult life. CFM instilled in me a respect for life... As a child, CFM taught me that barriers of race, creed or color are nonexistent when you walk in the footsteps of Jesus Christ."
> Raymond G. Murphy

The genius of CFM is affirming each person. Members and graduates, tens of thousands of them, attest to the electrifying discovery that they are important, gifted people of God, needed to work for peace and justice. Often, a surprised husband or wife exclaims "Who, me?" when told they are Christ acting in the world. The steady study of Scripture, listening to the call of the Gospel, underlines the dignity and responsibility of every member.

Faithful clergy have been partners with couples, proclaiming a viable people-theology. Father Joseph Payne, John Coffield, Ed Hogan, Bill Nerin, Don Kanaly, Charles Buswell, Frank Hurley, the brothers Ed and Fran Eschweiler, movement chaplains Jerry Fraser and Ed Kohler, Paul Valente, Bill McNulty, Pete Sammon, John Garcia, John Dietzen, Brian Joyce, Dennis Geaney, Bill McMahon, Ed

Hallem, Francis Syrianey, Bill Peters, Joseph Munier, Bill Clark and Louis Putz never ceased to encourage families to analyze their life experience in Gospel terms, even as they themselves did likewise. Later, Charles Buswell became bishop of Pueblo, Colorado, and Frank Hurley became bishop of Alaska.

Fathers John Garcia and Peter Sammon of the San Francisco Bay Area began the experiment of CFM early on, encouraging couples to involvement and leadership.

Father Garcia constantly challenged the CFM leadership and chaplains to go out to the poor and bring them into the movement. From his experience in the CFM groups in his parish, which included couples from many different backgrounds, he saw this as a priority for depth and effectiveness in CFM.

Peter Sammon watched many CFM children grow up and enter politics, question militarism and the Vietnam War, become advocates for the poor. Director of the Family Life Office in San Francisco, he recommended that a couple take over his role. Peg and Ed Gleason of the CFM continue to be advocates and educators for families.

When the subject of sanctuary for refugees from Central America became a priority in Father Sammon's own life, he did not force the issue on parishioners. The people of St. Theresa Parish were invited to spend a year together, with their pastor and Sister Kathleen Healey, in prayer and study to discern the movement of the Holy Spirit in their lives.

> The question is not Sanctuary as such. The real question is, "Can we be open to asking the question, What is is the Gospel of Jesus saying to us?' The process of decision-making is at the heart of Christian life and the *community* needs to ask the question, in prayer and faith, and come to a decision. The process of Observe-Judge-Act is the best way to get people involved. Most often, the question is asked, "Is it legal?" That is not the question. The question is regard for the struggle of life; the preservation of

life is sacred.

In my life as a priest, the CFM Conventions at Notre Dame put me in touch with the great prophetic voices of our time, ten years ahead of the church. Monsignor Hillenbrand saw so clearly that the work of the laypeople is doing Christ's work in the marketplace. He was a great influence on my thinking. He taught us to ask the right questions always. Most people just want to know what the "bottom line" is, but that does not ask the question, does not form consciences."

Father Dan Cipar reflected:

I never asked who is my neighbor ... I knew we were supposed to love everybody.... During a discussion at a CFM meeting of this 'obvious question,' I learned the answer, not in the general terms of theology, but in the world of actual people, in the concrete realities of their lives. They talked about real people — neighbors in need ... a local paper carrier, a good student with a scientific mind, who needed financial help for school. The CFMers decided to help him get aid. CFM has given me a deeper understanding of the Body of Christ, influenced my consciousness of how much the Sacraments I administer mean to families. I now give Communion to a father, a mother, rather than a man or woman .... I have learned to give a sermon on patience with reference to living in a family.

Searching the Scriptures together, observing and analyzing situations, families and chaplains realized all of life is one, undifferentiated, to be lived in union with Christ. Facing the fragmentation in the world, the CFMers' own brokenness could be acknowledged and healed.

Father Joseph Payne, CSC, pastor of Little Flower Church in South Bend, Indiana, was one of the first pastors to welcome CFM in the parish.

Father Gerald Weber, reflecting on his long involvement with CFM, says we anticipated by thirty years what the church now says should be the role of the laity:

We cannot go back, but what we learned can be very helpful for the present moment. We discovered people want to wrestle with the Gospel in their own life. We learned the dangers and pitfalls in small communities, they are tremendously supportive, but can become exclusive. We need to be open to new and different kinds of people. We must beware of elitism in the church. For a lawyer and a bricklayer to be in the same group is an opportunity to learn from each other."

Another priest reflects:

CFM led me into the Civil Rights Movement. Our biblical study changed my preaching, exposed me to new thinking. The biggest obstacle to Christianity is religion. Religion is doing, helping people to help themselves. We confuse Christian love with rescuing.

Chaplains and people formed secure friendships. Bernie Rachel writes in *ACT*:

This is a fitting time for this letter. Father Bill O'Neill was ordained in 1961, twenty-five years ago. He is one of those special persons who loves his work, loves people and has supported CFM throughout his priesthood. He is everywhere at once — at the CFM Convention he helped us win the Trivial Pursuit Tournament, took his turn as hall monitor during one of the nightly gatherings. His favorite saying is, "God sends his gift wrapped in people."

Before Father Bill arrived in our parish I had never heard of CFM. I am thankful for God's special gifts wrapped up in Father Bill and my CFM family.

Father Ed Hamel admits Dennis Geaney got him into CFM. He remembers being on the phone with CFMers in Park Forest, Illinois, planning sessions, family liturgies, and picnics. Monsignor Hillenbrand was a power figure in the formation of CFM. Many were the fights between the Program Committee and their mentor; always diplomatically handled by the Bonsignores, Joe and Madelyn. The sparks flew, but so too were the flames of CFM living keenly alive. We need to heed voices of new prophets though their prophecies are often harsh. If the movement wishes to live, it must heed the voices.

Dennis Geaney is one of the prophets:

> Our neighbor is just as much the people of India facing a drought as the poor person who comes to the door for a handout. One way to bind up the wounds of the world is to enact better U.S. immigration laws. We condemn birth control, but we refuse to lift a finger to help countries that have problems. Our neighbor is the American people who need enlightened and honest information.

The manual, *CFM and the Priest*, served as the basic chaplain's book until Father Ed Kohler noted that nuns, brothers, lay theologians, experienced CFM couples, seminarians, and those who had left the religious life serve as chaplains. As other Christian churches joined CFM, their clergy became chaplains. Perhaps we will have to find a new word to embrace all those who serve in this role.

Prophet-chaplain Louis Putz, now over seventy years of age, retired from a forty-year span of University teaching and as Rector of Moreau Seminary in South Bend, Indiana, in the 1970s. Undaunted by passing years, this energetic dreamer began a movement for seniors, based on the Observe-Judge-Act method he had promoted all his life in the Young Christian Student and Christian Family Movements.

> The basic reason I dreamed of Harvest House is that we're not alone in the aging process and we need one another more than ever to continue celebrating life and being useful to society. Older cultures like the Oriental and the European have considerably more respect for white hair and wrinkled brow than Americans who generally shelve old people as non-productive. I am convinced there is a wealth of human resources available among the retired and semi-retired. They have precious experience, professional skills, talents and, most of all, time.

Harvest House, together with The Forever Learning Institute that Father Putz founded, uses a leadership ministry of the elderly to the elderly. In the Fort Wayne-South Bend area of Indiana, more than 3,000 members are served. The Harvest House dream has moved into other parts of the country.

Thousands of couples repeat, "Life can never be the same." Observe-Judge-Act is a way of life, as is reading the Gospel in the light of the 20th century. Couples assumed remarkable roles as they broke out of their cocoons. Pat and Patty Crowley exemplified this emerging laity. Indefatigable in generosity of time, energy and worldly goods in the service of others, they were modern-day apostles. Recipients of the Pontifical Pro Ecclesia et Pontifice medal, they were a model for all CFMers. When Pat died in 1974, he was mourned by rich and poor alike, brothers and sisters whom he had included in his loving orbit.

In 1982 Patty was awarded the U.S. Catholic Award for "Furthering the Cause of Women in the Church." The award cited her work as co-president of CFM, as papal advisor, and as a Christian in the marketplace. "Patty," noted the award, "brought new power and dignity to the roles of laywoman, wife and mother."

At a talk on the importance of Vatican II, Cardinal John Dearden remembered Pat and Patty's involvement at a winter meeting of lay consultants, called by a committee to draft the Council's document "The Church in the Modern World." "Pat and Patty made a real contribution," the Cardinal said. "The potential of the chapters on the family and peace are still not realized ... because our society needs to make a cultural leap before we can understand the basic Christian ideas of community." The CFMers were making this countercultural leap.

When Ray and Dorothy Maldoon followed the Crowleys as President-couple of CFM, in the early '70s, they assumed the task of steering the movement through troubled waters. The upheaval in the church after Vatican II triggered an unprecedented exodus of priests, sisters and laypeople. The revolution of ideas, the changes in society deeply affected families. Ray and Dorothy, gifted with the ability to encourage and lead, kept CFM moving in a time of transition. Involved in every important CFM action, they were leaders in their community, laying the groundwork for a massive ongoing program of friendship with, and assistance to, migrant families. In tune with the thrust of Vatican II, they encouraged the National Committee to turn its attention to developing ecumenical CFM groups.

The CFM couples learned the benefits of working and acting together. The training, through the methodology of the yearly program, prepared all of them to be leaders in their field. Barbara and Armando Carlo work at Angel Guardian Senior Center in Chicago. "The CFM," they say, "played an important part in our life and we are thankful for its philosophy and the people who made it so meaningful. We went from CFM to leadership in the Marriage Encounter ... a complementary tool for CFM and vice-versa. CFM prepared us for the leadership we were to go into in the future, for the personal crises we were to face later; it nourished our spiritual life and our sense of being the Church."

Ray and Eleanor Ensroth have been CFMers for twenty-four of their twenty-nine years of married life. They took their children on CFMMV vacations in Appalachia, hosted students from Mexico, France, India, Indonesia. Members of their Archdiocesan Pastoral Council, Eleanor and Ray are eucharistic ministers. Two of their married daughters and their husbands are new members of CFM. Ray and Eleanor model the priority of family values passing from generation to generation. "CFM is a way of life, helping us develop spiritually, socially and emotionally in the atmosphere of extended family love."

The saga of the Tomanto family can be repeated many times, with a different backdrop. In 1958, Father Leo O'Brien knocked on the door of the young couple and invited them to join CFM. "When we asked him what it was all about," they remember, "he said, 'Just come see!'" Bob and Irene say that since that day years ago, "CFM has been a motivating force in our lives and the lives of our children." With Father Ed Cantwell, they created a Cana marriage preparation program. At the same time, the thirty-year-old husband of a CFM family died suddenly of a heart attack. He left a widow and seven children — and a pile of building materials for an addition to their home. The Tomanto action group worked together to rebuild the house for Joan and the children.

Moving to Hawthorne, New York, they met Monsignor Bob Fox of Full Circle. In awe, they say, "Only a visionary like Bob would ask ten couples of CFM to recruit ten thousand others for his 'Thing in the Spring,' a renovation plan for the inner city of New York. People came from city and suburbs alike to sweep and paint and learn and grow together as they reached out to one another amid the riots of East Harlem."

Again, "Action built on action and we spent summer vacations in Appalachia. We remember Annie Page, widow of a West Virginia miner, blind, in her eighties, living in a shack and telling us 'how much God loved us.'"

Eventually, Bob and Irene were New York Federation Couple, then Area leaders. "Life was sweet," Irene writes, "then, the bubble burst. Bob's company went out of business and he found a job in Florida. It wasn't planned, it happened. The old loneliness — the same need for family and friends led us again to CFM."

It took the Tomantos a while to adjust to the move. "We spent months observing Miami. It is a city of contrasts — very wealthy homes and very poor migrants, a city of divorce and remarriage, of impersonal shopping centers and little opportunity to build community ... Miami is a taste of the future. It has been an uncomfortable taste but, three years later, we are home again with new people in CFM."

Bill and Mary Kay Vogel have been CFMers for ten years. Bill is an active member in his church, the Lord of Life Lutheran Church. Mary Kay is a member of St. Cecilia's

Roman Catholic Church. Concerned about the Boat People of Vietnam, the Vogels, together with their CFM group, sponsored the Nynh family and went on to sponsor another refugee family. Bill and Mary Kay have adopted three Korean children, Andy, Susanne and Daniel, to be with Gretchen and Elizabeth. Committed to their families and the community, Bill delivers Meals on Wheels and Mary Kay is a leader in the La Leche League, originally founded by CFM wives in the early years of CFM.

Actions begin and become a part of life. Joe and Lee Saunders have been in CFM for more than twenty-eight years. They've been Foreign Student Representatives for the Detroit Federation for eighteen years. They took part in a simple action to host foreign students and at one time hosted fifty-two in their home! Joe has acted as father of the bride for a young friend from India. The Saunders keep close ties with Wayne State University, placing foreign students with families whenever needed. There are ten children in their family, and yet students and clergy from the world over have once called the Saunders' house "home."

Ralph and Reggie Weissert of South Bend, Indiana, have been CFMers for over thirty-five years. Participating in a seminar on pastoral theology at Holy Redeemer College, they told their audience:

> We learned the Observe-Judge-Act approach ... to analyze critically situations in the light of the Gospel and act on that analysis. When we were studying racial conflict, one family in our group moved into a changing neighborhood and opened their home to unwed mothers-to-be. The father in this family was working as an engineer on defense projects. He decided, in conscience, he could no longer work to design weapons of destruction and quit his job, taking a much lower paying one. This was a courageous example to many of us. Several of the CFM families adopted racially mixed children. The decision was not easy.... They were criticized by both blacks and whites.
>
> We had a black teenager as part of our family for a

time. In our middle-class, suburban area, we were the only ones who entertained blacks and foreigners. We and our children were accused of being "nigger-lovers." Our work with foreign students at Notre Dame and St. Mary's gave our children an understanding that hopes and aspirations, discouragements and pain are the same for all people the world over. We believe these examples (not for boasting) are an indication that attitudes in a family are developed in company with other families, over a long period of time ... day by day, week by week.

Families must have some kind of support group to enable them to serve the wider community.... When we marched silently in tribute to Martin Luther King Jr., at his death, the children walking with their families and others knew what they were doing was witnessing to the kinship of families in a time of distress.

The incredible networking, the weaving together of families, took place daily. Shari and Bob Bauchat, who went to Brazil, sent back news of the "grim reality" of life for the people and how they started a CFM group. Father Bill Eckert, also living and working in Brazil, wrote in the seventies of the "two different worlds":

> The economic situation is a disaster. It is in a terrible state ... with an inflation rate of more than 112 percent. The poor suffer terribly - the mad rush for "development" is leaving this country more and more in debt ... payments that will influence generations of future Brazilians.
>
> The Church would make you proud .... It is a real support and hope for the poor ... involved in justice and peace ... It brings a good deal of tension but it is a testimony that makes one glad to be a part of it.

In Moline, Illinois, the roots of the Blackhawk Federation families go back to 1955 when Father Edward F. Fitton of Sacred Heart Parish contacted the Crowleys for information about CFM. Building an ever-larger community of families, interacting in communal celebrations, camp-outs and community actions they got acquainted with neighbors, minorities, elected politicians, got involved in parish activities and sponsored Cuban refugee families.

The CFMers established FISH to give emergency aid to the needy, Birthright to provide emergency pregnancy services, and worked also at the Catholic Worker House. In 1982, sparked by CFMer Carolyn McGuire, families started working with the Special Olympics Bowling Project. The families of the Blackhawk Federation know CFM is not an organization — it is people. People of courage, faith, trust and who dare to reflect God's love in serving others.

Frank and Pat Gacnik typify the effect of CFM formation over a period of time. They write:

> CFM radically changed the course of our lives. From complete non-involvement we found ourselves helping at political meetings, community open house meetings ... It has taken us and our family into situations we would never have considered — migrant labor camps, nursing homes, poverty community centers, tutoring programs, leadership positions in parish, school, archdiocese, 4-H, Great Books Program, low-income housing corporations, crusades at the state capitol to protest abortion. But *also* small actions: family prayers, discussions, celebrations, welcoming new neighbors, greeting a new person at church. We've been involved at Lookout Mountain School for boys, a juvenile institution for boys from ages fourteen to eighteen.
>
> Once, a burly young man, with the toughness of more than his sixteen years, stood up and said, "Everyone thinks we're goof-offs and not worth much, but you've made us feel as if maybe we can do something." Something unheard of was happening. These boys were not supposed to be caring, or thankful. They had been sentenced for car stripping, theft or assault. Society said they were tough hoods and teenage rebels; yet love can break down barriers. The party, an annual event, is a culmination of the year's programs of bimonthly visits and activities. A CFMer can remember that "we have the most famous criminal in history as our leader and he said: 'when I was in prison, you visited me.'"
>
> A healthy Christian family life is the most important part of life, yet most lacking in our society. There is little

recognition of this by those in the family life field ... CFM helped us learn skills and the art of group leadership, experience the support of real community, beautiful liturgies and celebrations, unique, rewarding relationships with priests and sisters — and the enrichment of our own marriage.

Yet, CFM is no panacea ... We'll have problems with one another and within our families. CFM can never eliminate problems, but can give us the skills, strength and faith to cope and that is a rare commodity. For us, CFM is a life-style. It taught us to become aware of situations and ask two questions: 'What is our Christian response? What can we do about them?' It is not just talk but *do*. Once learned, O-J-A can never be forgotten. If we could leave our children just one thing, it would be a life of commitment to Gospel values ... They have to see their parents' faith become vital and real.

The Aldriches are a CFM prophet-family. Their ten children are all involved in "non-exploitive" work. Janet and Bob have authored a book, *Children and Non-Violence*, published by Hope Publishing Company in Pasadena, CA. Their story is recounted by Bob:

> Significant changes started for us with the doorbell's ring in 1957. Newly moved to Santa Clara and strangers in the parish, we were welcomed to a Christian Family Movement meeting. Soon we were involved in a "For Happier Families" group — sharing experiences on raising children and gaining new insights on church teachings.
>
> Learning constructive means of discipline and providing for shared experiences with the children were valuable to us. Communication and family meetings were indispensible. This family-oriented first year appealed to our needs as parents of a young family. The techniques of Observe-Judge-Act, jokingly referred to as snoop, gossip, and indulge were teaching us to make informed decisions. We enjoyed these discussions and social encounters and soon became quite comfortable in our group.
>
> CFM planners, however, were well aware of the apathy

comfort can breed. Much to our dislike, but later appreciation, we were shuffled with other groups in the parish for the second year. Now we were investigating the social milieu — the wider community of society with which our family so intimately interacts. We were led beyond the doorstep while we would have preferred the familiarity of our home. Sharing with those in need did not become a fulfilling experience and contact with our less fortunate brothers and sisters left a lasting impression.

CFM also prepared us well for church renewal in the wake of Vatican Council II. What had been avant-garde liturgical experimentation by CFM became normal practice. We participated more fully in the parish adult education program and, later, in church renewal at various other levels.

In CFM, there was more annual regrouping and further delving into the political aspects of our environment. More discomfort was felt and it was about this time that a good friend remarked that he found being uncomfortable was a sign to give attention. We did pay attention and our life as a family changed dramatically. The spiritual learnings came home to roost in a very profound way.

Designing nuclear missiles at Lockheed brought financial gratification, but we gradually became ill at ease with such a means of support. Taking our friend's advice, we did pay attention — we "observed" what was taking place; all the ramifications of that deadly endeavor; the misuse of money and talent. We also studied other opportunities which would reap a livelihood.

Then we "judged." We discussed our dilemma at family meetings in true CFM style. The children were brought into the decision-making process as much as possible. We investigated and evaluated many things — the impact of our lifestyle and how it could change, the children's opportunities to be more active as family members, how our friends would react, and much more.

Finally, all this observing and judging led to its inevitable conclusion — "action." Both of us changed our primary occupations and revised our roles in the family. The fulfilling work we are now doing — Janet working with minority children in public schools and Bob in research and education on the effects of militarism in the world — was in no small way influenced by our CFM years. CFM was our basic training course in Christianity. One important thing it inculcated in us is that being a Christian is not a comfortable vocation, but it is certainly fulfilling.

Pat Foley writes:

Ministry to families can take many forms. I volunteer weekly at a crisis center and shelter for battered women and their children. I was first introduced to Women's Center and Shelter (WC&S) through CFM. At a leaders' meeting prior to the 1978 Area IV Convention in Pittsburgh, we were taken to different sections of the city on what was called an "exposure trip." Some groups went to senior citizens centers, some to soup kitchens; I went to WC&S. I remember feeling disbelief that a crisis center for women was needed. I felt very uncomfortable that afternoon, but was able to put the whole afternoon way down deep in my heart.

I kept it locked up for a couple of years until one Sunday when I was reading the Volunteers Needed column in the press. I noticed WC&S requesting help with their Children's Program. I was still able to ignore it. At least until the following Sunday when CBS aired a segment on a crisis center in Texas and the whole subject of wife abuse. A very wise person once told me, "If something hits you three times, you can almost bet it's the Holy Spirit and you better respond to it." I could no longer ignore the message. Like Simon of Cyrene, I reluctantly went to WC&S to help.

One of the most common forms that domestic violence takes is wife battering. Statistics show that a woman is beaten every eighteen seconds in our country; from a minimal slap or as vicious as broken bones, loss of teeth, eyes, and even murder. The stories of abuse I hear from women and the knowledge of what children have seen sometimes make it hard for me to continue. Each story is the worst I've heard until I return the following week. The only thing that has changed is that I no longer go to the shelter reluctantly. Now I go eagerly, knowing I will be needed. I thank CFM for introducing me to WC&S. If my group never comes up with an action, I still get mine done each week.

In 1973, anthropologist Margaret Mead invited the couples from the Executive Committee of the International Confederation of Christian Family Movements to a conference at Tarrytown, New York. The meeting would include a group of experts and resource persons from various fields connected with family life.

Dr. Mead had met Pat and Patty Crowley, heard from them about CFM, and was intrigued by the idea of husbands and wives working together on common concerns. Margaret Mead saw the Christian Family Movement as a modern expression of an extended family building friendship across the barriers of race, continents, and classes. She told the group:

> This question of grouping people with common problems together and their relationship with the rest of society is very important now. Are they going to be a leaven for the rest of society or are they just going to thrive on their own strengths and leave the rest of society out? It seems to me that unless you have a family that is working well as a resource and strength for a whole group of people, it isn't doing a great deal for the group today.

At another time during the conference, she said:

> The loneliest people in the world are people who are married to somebody they can't talk to. As I see it, CFM provides people a wider context by which they can become acquainted with their husbands and wives and developing a pair who can do all kinds of wonderful things together. The main thing the couple producing children do is to be the focal point of creating the kind of life for those children which produces the kind of people society needs. The chief thing the family needs is human relationships.

The meeting at Tarrytown dealt with the topic, "Friendship: Families' Answer to Loneliness in the World." During the discussion, Mary Conway Kohler, former San Francisco Juvenile Judge commented, "If I had only known of an organization like CFM years ago, I can't tell you what it would have meant to me."

Antonio and Christina Alcocer of Mexico, representing eighteen Latin American countries, reported:

> We are calling on CFM to serve all families, including "incomplete families." CFM must include unmarried mothers, single adoptive parents, common-law marriages, and even parentless children. Despite the disapproval of militaristic governments, CFM remains vital because it consciously attracts working-class families.

The biggest concern expressed by Edi and Mary Magdalena Barnor of Ghana, representatives of Africa were: "Apartheid in South Africa and the need for the church in Africa to permit the development of an indigenous Christianity."

Communication between the groups of CFMers and the resource group of sociologists, psychologists and psychiatrists was not always clear, and criticism of CFM was freely expressed. The chasm separating the two groups at the beginning of the weekend was pinpointed by one of the psychologists who said: "Your initials — CFM — represent to me the very things I am against. Christian, family, movement." It was a forthright statement and laid out in the open the separation existing within the conference. Where would the grass-roots couples and the experts meet?

Margaret Mead laid the foundation for agreement: the overriding concern of all participants for a healthy family life. She called attention to the fact that loneliness haunts people who live in an industrial society from the cradle to the grave because people lack the familiar and spiritual ties to one another. She reminded the group that older people have left the American home, relegated to golden ghettoes, which leaves young couples left to fend for themselves just when they most need the protection of a larger, extended family. Grandparents can best bridge the gap between the generations because, having seen the most change, they can change the most. The anthropologist said it was important in a healthy society for several generations to live together.

By the end of the weekend the chasm had closed. The group of CFM couples, professionals, resource-people, had grown very close by sharing projects, dreams, failures, and hopes for the future of family life. Even though we were diverse in background, experience and philosophy, we were, each of us, standing in a different place, looking at the same sun.

The genius of CFM allows people to learn to affirm each other's gifts. A people-theology is evolving as women and men assume responsibility for themselves and for each other. Theology is to be lived. The CFMers recognize that the admonition to feed the hungry, comfort the sorrowing, free the oppressed, are not pious phrases but a terrifying call to integrate the words of Scripture with life. In small communities, the continuing challenge is to contemplate reality and to move into action. CFMers learn that life is not simple as they care for refugees, embrace children of war, bind the wounds of battered women, shelter the homeless, nurture teenagers. Barriers do break down "when you walk in the footsteps of Jesus Christ."

CHAPTER VIII
A New Moment

> "We need one another ... we are responsible for one another ... what we do affects everyone."
> "Your Family Called to Action," 1980

When the U.S. bishops declared 1980s "The Decade of the Family," a new moment arrived for CFM. The call validated the concern for families shown by CFM since its inception. CFM had found its roots in the graced vision of Cardinal Joseph Cardijn in the conviction that people ministering to each other could change society. It was this vision which Pope John XXIII stressed when he said:

> Discussion of Scripture and Liturgy are essential to apostolic growth. Ignorance of Scripture is ignorance of Christ, the Way, the Truth, and Life and deprives members of a tool for their spiritual progress and for action. Action does not precede development. They take place simultaneously.

The threat of nuclear war, the ever-widening disparity between the haves and the have-nots, the specter of death by starvation, the disintegration of family life call for serious education and action. Since the '40s CFM has encouraged small groups of couples to come together to earnestly study Scripture, look at the world with penetrating eyes and take action for improvement. The interconnectedness of every human person, of all that is in the world, is the thrust of CFM programs.

The Social Inquiries have knit into one garment all the pressures that impinge on family life: relationships, community structures, human rights, war and peace, economic justice, the needs of the elderly, the disenfranchised and the oppressed. Highlighting the call of the Gospel, the two major encyclicals of the 20th century, Pope John XXIII's *Mater et Magistra* and *Pacem in Terris*, and the documents of the Second Vatican Council, CFM programs formed a generation of families committed to bringing about nonviolent social change.

In this new moment of the eighties, declared the Decade of the Family by the U.S. bishops, CFM continues to emphasize the importance of families acting together for peace and justice.

Executive Directors Kay and Gary Aitchison of Ames, Iowa, are a permanent deacon-couple in the Archdiocese of Dubuque. They say:

> Joining CFM ten years ago was the beginning of a new life. It led us out of stagnation, often made us feel uncomfortable, prodded us to grow, change and become more than we dreamed. We found friends, shared with each other, gained confidence to share more of ourselves with our family, group and the world around us. Christ came alive in our marriage and our home. The CFM took us from small actions to a Mission Vacation with mountain people in Kentucky and Tennessee. We established a pilot series of ecumenical marriage seminars in our community. The CFM of the future must continue to arouse a concern for peace and justice, as well as a more simple lifestyle in its member-couples, as well as in society.

The 1980s brought new life to the movement, report Dan and Judy Printz of Chicago. "We've discovered a new trend in groups. We are reaching second-generation CFMers who join because the movement was such a good part of their childhood."

When CFM members around the country were asked to comment on issues they would like to see included in

future programs, they responded:
- More Christ-centeredness
- A commitment to witness
- An awareness of persons rather than labels (e.g., poor, divorced, clergy)
- Sustain social consciousness and actions
- Help families become agents of social change
- Promote caring communities who act together on a local and national level

A group of CFM teenagers, long involved in actions with their parents, have designed their own Inquiry book: *In Search of Jesus: An Action Book for Teens*. The young authors, Bonsignores, Fishers, Zellners, Mary Kay Gacnik, Christine Reiber, Kristin Tomanto and Michael Zypasek, developed an enticing model of discovery for their peers. Following Cardijn's pattern of Scripture study, the social inquiry, analysis and action, the book is written with simplicity and warmth. Meetings confront the basic questions of life: "Who am I? Who is Jesus? How do I share with others?" Confidently the writers lead their associates into challenging areas, "We are the Church, Sharing the Good News, We Can Make a Difference." In "Sharing the Good News" these young CFMers outline serious concepts:

Opening Prayer:
Son, you will never succeed in putting enough love
into the heart of man and into the world,
For man and the world are hungry for an infinite love,
And God alone can love with a boundless love.
But if you want, son, I give you my Life.
Draw it within you.
I give you my heart, I give it to my sons.
Love with my heart,
And all together you will feed the world,
and you will save it.
Michel Quoist — *Prayers*
Sheed and Ward, New York

Reports of Action from previous meeting

Scripture:
This has taught us love — that he gave up his life for us; and we, too, ought to give up our lives for our brothers. If a man who was rich enough in this world's goods saw that one of his brothers was in need, but closed his heart to him, how could the love of God be living in him? My children our love is not to be just words or mere talk, but something real and active...

1 John 3:16-18
The Jerusalem Bible

Discussion:
What is meant by the phrase "we, too, ought to give up our lives for our brothers?" How does the presence of God's love affect us and those around us?

Social Inquiry:
Lord, why did you tell me to love all men, my brothers?
I have tried, but I come back to you, frightened...

You have forced me to open my door.
Like a squall of rain in the face, the cry of men
has awakened me.
Outside, men were lying in wait for me.
I did not know they were so near, in this house,
in this street, in this office;
my neighbor, my colleague, my friend.
As soon as I started to open the door I saw them,
with outstretched hands, anxious eyes,
longing hearts, like beggars on Church steps...

Don't worry, God says, you have gained all.
While men came in to you,
I, your father,
I, your God,
Slipped in among them.

Michel Quoist
Prayers
Sheed and Ward, New York

Observe:
Teenagers are a very special part of the church today; they have a very special purpose. Discuss with your parents

A New Moment

and some friends what the role of the teenager in the church is and what can be done to make this role more vital.

Judge:

1. How can you use your own special talents to play a more important role in the church?
2. How can you encourage more teenagers to become interested in their religion?...to play an active role in the church?
3. Do you feel it is an obligation to be involved in your parish or church?

Act

Suggestion:

Use your special talents as a group and as individuals to interest more teenagers in their religion. One possibility is to organize a fun-filled spiritual evening activity to encourage teens to share and grow with you. Use this meeting to encourage these other teens to form a group like yours. You will need to guide their progress and help them along the way.

Some Other Ideas To Get Teens Interested

1. Serve coffee, milk and donuts to families after Sunday services. Set up a table where teens can learn more about the program.
2. Arrange for teens to speak at church services.
3. Visit a church other than your own and invite their teens to join you.
4. Ask each member of your group to recruit two of their friends.

Prepare for the Next Meeting:

You may wish to make assignments for the "Observers."

Closing Prayer

Pass It On

It only takes a spark to get a fire going.
And soon all those around can warm up in its glowing.
That's how it is with God's love,

Once you've experienced it,
You spread His love to everyone
You want to pass it on...

Kurt Kaiser — *Songs*
San Anselmo, California.

In its first seven months, 800 copies of *In Search of Jesus* were ordered by people from all over the country.

The closing meeting of *In Search of Jesus* is a celebration of friendship and a commissioning into action: "It's Glorious to Be Alive!"

Stretching the boundaries for CFM families continues to be the goal of the CFM programs. For the eighties, the melange includes Marriage the Great Adventure; Revaluing Christian Commitment; Discovering Others; Love Happens in Families; Work, Money and Your Family; Quality of Life Renewed; The Eve of Orwell: A Christian Response to a Brave New World; Families Called to Action; Understanding and Building Community; Peacemaking; and Family Values in the Marketplace.

During the U.N. World Refugee Year, families were resettled, children adopted. In the U.N. Year of the Family the ICCFM and the World Council of Churches brought together families from fifty-one countries to face their common concerns, in order to commit themselves to social change.

The CFM house organ, *ACT*, keeps up a running report of actions. One story reports the saga of George and Carol Ann Hochbrueckner, who reflect that encountering CFM in the '60s in the formative days of their marriage set the pattern for all aspects of their future life:

> CFM opened up and nourished our perspective as individuals, as a couple, as parents and as members of society, all within the framework of the Mystical Body. We were young, in love and eager for the many challenges CFM offered. The variety of subjects dealt with over the years helped give us a keener sense of who we were and how we

could use our talents. The technique of Observe, Judge and Act, while simple, is perhaps the most brilliant formula to produce change that one could devise ... It is in the political sphere that we have given the bulk of our time, energy and commitment. Our initial involvement in politics was in California, the result of a CFM action — nonpartisan voter registration and getting out the vote. Prior to this, we had never considered participation in politics, other than voting. We had both been raised in very nonpolitical families. George, at the time, was pursuing a career in engineering ... It was during the Kennedy funeral we vowed to intensify our commitment to the political world ... When we moved back east in 1970, we were initially disheartened by the lack of participation by the Catholic community in the political process ... a direct contrast to our experiences in our California CFM community. CFM had not only authenticated and elevated participation in politics, but actually put this pursuit in the realm of a Christian's responsibility....

George ran for the New York state assembly against a popular but ineffective nine-year incumbent. We won by almost three thousand votes. Our experiences over these ten years have reaffirmed our belief that government can have a tremendous impact on the quality of life for all people ... In the 1986 election George became a member of the U.S. Congress. The principles CFM taught us so many years ago have held us in good stead. It is those values that have continued to sustain and nourish us for over twenty years.

Twelve-year-old Gretchen Vogel was second-place winner in an essay contest. She interviewed two senior citizens, contrasting their lives with life today. Interviewing Mrs. Bess Ferguson, eighty-six years old, and her own great-grandmother Mrs. Loretta Schultz, eighty-seven years old, Gretchen makes some good observations:

> I think parents are not as strict now as they were seventy years ago and both ladies agreed ... When asked if she thought life for young people is easier now, Mrs. Ferguson thought young people have similar problems and

concerns, just handle them differently ... Grandma thought life is easier now because kids don't have to work so hard.

Mrs. Ferguson said they were five and six when they started to school but it wasn't unusual to have fifteen- or sixteen-year-old boys in the eighth grade because they could only go to school part of the year. They had ... to help on the farm the rest of the year. She also said there were no tests. Wouldn't that be wonderful?

I think life is harder now because of many reasons ... mainly because life is so much more complicated. It seems life was so much simpler then.

And there were other stories about CFMers:

■ Dan Van Belleghem, John Mallon and Tom Ricks attended the United States Catholic Conference annual meeting for diocesan social action directors and noted in *ACT:* "We learned that twenty percent of the U.S. population earns about forty-four percent of the national income, and that twenty percent earns only slightly more than four percent ... Bishop John McCarthy of Texas told a group that he has become more and more concerned about living the Gospels and deepening his awareness of social issues." Tom reports the bishop feels that he and his fellow bishops "are being put in boxes. When bishops speak out on the right to life, they are right wing ... When they condemn poverty, they are called bleeding-heart liberals ... When they address the issue of nuclear war, they become the dupes of Moscow, and when they support Poland, they are tools of the State Department. Yet our main concern today must be the poor, the homeless, the imprisoned."

"Technically, none of us were social action directors," Dan said, "but CFM has a long history of social action. I feel this should be more in the province of the laity. Most of the attendees indicated social action is still being done by clergy and religious.

This could be a good area of debate in CFM ...

with discussion in *ACT*."

- Editors Tom and Vernie Dale noted the ICCFM meeting in Mexico where Cardinal Paolo Evaristo Arns of Sao Paulo, Brazil, spoke on the "theology of poverty." The ICCFM delegates attended meetings of the small groups called base communities in Guadalajara, and national chaplain Father Jerry Fraser spoke to the assembly, encouraging them to use well the technique "that is ours — observe, judge, act ... to use it with the sense of extending our families outward, showing God's love, serving others, creating God's family and building the kingdom."

- On an update on the Foundation for International Cooperation, CFMers learn some of the history of FIC and are invited to join the latest Study Tour to Ireland, Scotland and Wales, where travelers will stay "with families, sometimes CFMers."

- Sue and Wayne Hamilton of Michigan are President-couple in the late eighties. Their enthusiasm for CFM is contagious. Sue Hamilton was the first woman to run for village president in her small community of Manchester, Michigan. Sue didn't win, maybe because she would not miss the CFM winter board meeting to stay home and campaign.

- Vince Barlow, well-known for the inspiration he gave teenagers at National Conventions, produced "Head and Heart," an album of his songs.

- Bob and LaVerne Sober assume their new role as editors of *ACT*.

By telling their stories, CFMers keep each other connected with their expanding family.

- The Blackhawk Federation lists in its newsletter skills available by CFMers who are out of work. They also donate money to their local food bank and the

Catholic Worker House.

- Monsignor Bill Peters told the CFM Board: "Family life directors are searching for quick ways to train people for family ministry. We're trying to do it all at once and are finding it is a much slower process." This director, from the Altoona-Johnstown Diocese in Pennsylvania, believes the CFM program is an ideal training ground for family ministers. "Parish family ministry teams need the support of a CFM group which has become a base community that reaches out to toch others in real life situations."

- A CFM mother, seriously ill and feeling helpless, found a new translation for the letters, CFM. She discloses: "CFM stands for Christian Family Meals."

- From Tina Sonneville in Rock Island, Illinois: "The neatest thing I can say about CFM is that our son and wife, married one year, will be moving back here and are looking forward to joining a CFM group. Our first CFM groups began twenty-five years ago. The Christian Family Movement touched our lives in many ways. Often the topic of discussion had not yet touched our lives, but it made us aware of others' problems. Or it was a topic we were struggling with and we found we were not alone. Leaders were formed in CFM by helping each of us develop our own potential. It has been a source of self-confidence, and as a support system it has been super. One of the few negative comments I've heard about CFM is that we should be actively involved in the anti-nuclear movement, not just sitting and discussing issues. I feel CFM is a place for everyone to discuss their views; then people can choose for themselves if they wish to be involved.

CFMers attend important meetings to talk about the philosophy of family life and involvement in the important issues of living as a Christian. The Hamiltons, Aitchisons,

Gacniks, Broerens, and many other CFM couples across the country are involved in Family Days, newspaper and magazine interviews, and conferences.

- In one of her newspaper columns, Dolores Curran told a story of CFM: "'We've discovered a great new group,' a young Florida couple told me. 'It's called the Christian Family Movement.' I smiled and told them that twenty-eight years ago my husband and I were part of a weekend for couples sponsored by the same CFM. They were surprised to learn that CFM is not a new, but a respected, mature movement which is experiencing new growth." As a result of Dolores' article, 100 requests for information about CFM were received at the National Office in Ames, Iowa.

- Father Ted Wolgamot, Director of the Office of Marriage and Family Life in Peoria, comes from a family of ten. He remembers when his parents, Pete and Marguerite Wolgamot, were involved in CFM in the '50s and '60s. In their house, he says, "CFM stood for Can't Find Mom."

- Alicia Valdes from the Movimiento Christiano in Dallas reflects: "You can't teach love to children if you cannot have love between spouses. Instead of saying Cinderella got married and lived happily ever after, it really should read, 'Cinderella got married and they tried every day.' You must work at a marriage. You can learn to be unhappy, but you can also learn to be happy."

- Father Jude Mili, still ministering in Appalachia, continues to invite CFM families to vacation and work in the towns of West Virginia.

- In the Philippines, President-couple Sito and Sony Sison report the 25th anniversary of CFM saying: "In the '70s, many CFMers in the Philippines were involved in the movement to construct a new Constitution for our country."

- In Michigan, the St. Lucy CFM experienced a Freedom Feast, combining the Passover Seder meal with Christ's freeing the people from the bondage of sin. Symbols of families' political, spiritual, or cultural bondage as individuals, as well as signs of freedoms, were used.

- Pat Foley works at a battered women's shelter and sees the major challenge facing the church and CFM as "helping find an answer to the question of what we are going to do with the new way of family living. This is a new time, in which many mothers are working people; people are tired when they get home. There is a major concentration on earning money to support families."

    Pat sees her own role as training families about battery. She says that fifty to sixty percent of battery of wives happens in the first year of marriage and that the church is not aware or willing to acknowledge it. "People can't face this reality as they can't face the problem of war because it is so ugly, especially in the suburban bubble."

    She continues: "There is a new problem for society — the new Meism which has lost sight of how to be family. We have lost the sense of family which helps us become more fully human. We are less human as a society."

- In Canada, CFMers continue their long tradition of action, helping establish a home for battered women, taking in Polish and Vietnamese families, and inviting school children to make 1,000 paper cranes, a symbol of peace and a reminder of the devastation of the nuclear bomb. The thousands of cranes are for display at the Hiroshima Peace Park in Japan.

- Fund-raising in Canada continues its unique success. The Canadian Department of Social Services granted CFM $3,000 in a recent year. When given the grant, the CFMers were told, "You are helping families as much as any of our organizations."

- In Oakland, California, two young people from CFM families were engaged to be married. Paul Smith and Miriam Walthers "can't help but have a good marriage, given the experiences and examples they've had being with many CFM families," says Kathleen Smith.

- From Mexico, Estelle and Mario Carota write to tell of the devastating inflation of more than 100 percent. It costs a half day's labor to buy one kilo of beans. The Carotas are involved in helping producing cooperatives which are completely owned and operated by the workers. They ask for present CFMers to help with the distribution of co-op products in the United States.

- A CFM mother says she respected the CFM people in her life because they were not overly pious and did not look on other people with an air of superiority. CFM, she says, taught everyone to have a compassionate heart.

It is a new moment in history. Young families, old-timers sense the call to deeper commitment. Father Warren Metzler, now national chaplain, gently prods the movement to keep confronting the hard issues of justice. When couples mourn the lack of chaplains, he suggests the best way to involve a priest or minister in CFM is "invite them to your parties. Let them see CFM is fun ... The development of meaningful relationships in and through CFM ... from the satisfaction of experiencing personal growth through involvement in important issues and actions in CFM. Most priests and ministers are longing for a place where they can be accepted for who they are. Treat him with respect, but treat him as an equal."

In good humor he reminds couples they have the

facility to call a group to prayer, to foster a comfortable and loving relationship with Scripture and to develop a sense of liturgical celebration through storytelling, blessings and feast-day parties.

Conscious of the critical moment of the eighties, Father Metzler says, "There's food, housing and resources out there — why can't the poor have them? ... We shouldn't get angry at people that are not there. Just gently remind them, keep on reminding them. Meaning lies in people, not ideas." Reflecting on the effects of the fear of nuclear war on children he tells CFMers "1986 is the ideal moment to explore the topic of peace, to realize our failure to sense its absence and how much we need it."

Coinciding with the United Nation Year of Peace in 1986, the Inquiry book *Peaceworks* based on Matthew 19:26 "...with God all things are possible" was offered to the membership. Authors of the book were the Foleys, Sobers, Wedoffs, Kaffenbergers, Hoffmans, Dennis Fernandez, Tim Eastly, Peter Ballo, and Warren Metzler. They noted:

> The Christian Family Movement presumes the dignity and value of every person; the need of everyone to communicate and care; the necessity for helping each other grow and fulfill our potential. People need people; families need families. We are all in this world, at this time in history, together.
>
> The person who does not march in a demonstration can be expressing a considered judgment as thorough as that of the person who does march. The important point is that both people have used their capacity for gathering fact, making judgments and taking action. This capacity to appraise situations without cracking up or "copping out" is especially needed in times of revolutionary ideas and actions. CFM has used the social inquiry method of Observe, Judge, and Act for many years simply because it *DOES* work in helping people develop their critical capacities.

Editors Jim and Pat Foley wrote:

> *Peaceworks* has been written to coincide with the

A New Moment

United Nation's International Year of Peace, 1986. We feel that it is time to look back to the early days of CFM and its relationship and commitment to social action. The climate of our society is such that a studied examination of the various aspects of peace is imperative. The basis for CFM's involvement in social action is justice. Paul VI reminds us "If you want peace, work for justice."

... It is the editor's premise that peace begins with the individual and spreads from there, as ripples in a pond, to the family, the community, and eventually throughout the world. Country to country, government to government, individual to individual — barriers to peace and the principles of *peaceworking* apply identically to each dyad. When we find that source of peace within the very centers of our beings, the God within each of us, indeed, "all things are possible."

Funk and Wagnall's Standard Desk Dictionary defines *Peace* as a state of mental or physical quiet or tranquillity; in a state or condition of order and harmony; the cessation of war; and *Work* as continued exertion or activity, whether physical or mental, directed to some purpose or end; that upon which labor is expended; to perform a function; to prove effective. Taken together, *Peaceworks* becomes the manifest destiny of each and every Christian.

Understanding that peace is more than the absence of war, some of the topics covered in *Peaceworks* were: Forgiveness, Winning and Competition, Anger, The Economics of the Arms Race, Nuclear Numbing, Peace in the Neighborhood, Battered Women, Pornography, Pro-Life, Fighting. The meetings "The War Within, The Kingdom Within"; and "Stereotypes and Isms" indicate the thrust of the Inquiries:

THE WAR WITHIN, THE KINGDOM WITHIN

Opening Prayer:

Is everyone involved in the action or actions of the group? Are all taking a turn in reporting their actions?

Reports

Reflection

"While you are proclaiming peace with your lips, be careful to have it more fully in your heart."
St. Francis Assisi

"If one of you is wise and understanding, let him show this in practice through a humility filled with good sense. Should you instead nurse bitter jealousy and selfish ambition in your hearts, at least refrain from arrogant and false claims against the truth. Wisdom like this does not come from above. It is earthbound, a kind of animal, even devilish, cunning. Where there are jealousy and strife, there are also inconstancy and all kinds of vile behavior. Wisdom from above, by contrast, is first of all innocent. It is also peaceable, lenient, docile, rich in sympathy and the kindly deeds that are its fruits, impartial and sincere. The harvest of justice is sown in peace for those who cultivate peace."
James 3:13-18
The New American Bible

"It is in each of us that the peace of the world is cast — in the frontiers of our hearts — from there it must be spread out to the limits of the universe."
Cardinal Leon Joseph Suenens

• What is the "wisdom from above" of which James speaks? How are we striving for it?

• How is peace a "harvest of justice"?

• How do the words of Suenens ring true regarding a connection between world peace and personal peace?

Social Inquiry: SHALOM is the Word

In an attempt to define inner peace, we quote an earlier CFM inquiry book titled *Shalom*: "The ancient Hebrew word "Shalom" (Peace) is a very rich word. Those who have Shalom are whole persons: they find fulfillment, security, prosperity, good health and relationships in daily living. They are intimately involved in humankind and are in tune with the whole divine ordering of the universe. Shalom is not a state, but something that is happening; a dynamic experience."

Chapter 4 of the letter of St. James asks "*What causes wars among us?*" It answers, "*Can't you see it is the passions at war within yourselves?*"

In a speech given in 1982, Sen. Mark Hatfield said, "We long for restoration within our own life, in relationship to others and with the Lord even as we are experiencing loneliness, alienation and exile. The peace we experience is piecemeal."

From Your Own Personal Experience, OBSERVE:

1. Describe someone you have known who has appeared to you to be in inner conflict. Describe your attitude and the attitude of others toward them at that time.
2. Have you ever met someone who seems to be free of inner struggles? Describe how their inner peace affected your attitude toward them at that time.
3. Describe a time when you felt a sense of inner peace. How did you arrive at this inner peace?

In Light of Christ's Teachings, JUDGE:

1. What causes the inner battles in our lives?
2. How does inner peace depend on outer circumstances?
3. What is most preventing us from achieving inner peace?
4. How can we cultivate inner peace?

From What Has Been Discussed, Decide How You Can ACT:

1. Consciously practice for one day removing from your life something which works against obtaining inner peace.
2. Experiment with inner peace through reaching out to others in action or in prayer.
3. Discuss some of the conclusions of tonight's meeting with others at home. Talk about the ways you can help each other achieve inner peace.

4. Create a quiet time/place in your home where you can further develop (reflect on) your inner peace.
5. Find out about and try "centering" prayer.

Before deciding on an action, read and reflect on the following:

All of the values we are promoting in this letter rest ultimately in the disarmament of the human heart and the conversion of the human spirit to God who alone can give authentic peace. Indeed, to have peace in our world, we must first have peace within ourselves. As Pope John Paul II reminded us in his 1982 World Day of Peace message, world peace will always elude us until peace becomes a reality for each of us personally. "It springs from the dynamism of free will guided by reason towards the common good that is to be attained in truth, justice and love." Inner peace becomes possible only when we have a conversion of the spirit. We cannot have peace with hate in our hearts.

The Challenge of Peace
God's Promise and our Response
A Pastoral Letter on War/Peace/N.C.C.B./U.S.C.C.

Write the **Act** you intend to do ... and share it with the group.

Look ahead to the **Observes** for the next meeting.

Closing Prayer:

Jesus, your love led you to suffer every burden imaginable. You promised us that all of our needs would be met by a caring Father who would never test us beyond our strength and who has a plan and a purpose for each of us. Help us to develop this conscious awareness of your love for us, so that the inner peace and a sense of meaning in our lives may be restored. As St. Augustine has written, "O God, you have made our hearts for yourself and we will be restless until we rest in you." Amen.

Peace Trivia

Did you know that . . .

In San Francisco, CA, a statue of that city's patron stands to address peace. Running as metallic veins through this sculpture are the melted guns of 2,000 San Franciscans who handed in their weapons after the assassination of Robert Kennedy. What weapons are concealed within us?

STEREOTYPES & ISMS: ARE THEY STILL WITH US?

Opening Prayer

Reports

Reflection

"If you want peace, work for justice."

Pope Paul VI

"Insult no man when he is old, for some of us, too, will grow old."

Sirach 8:7
New American Bible

A Samaritan woman came to draw some water, and Jesus said to her, "Give me a drink of water." (His disciples had gone into town to buy food.) The woman answered, "You are a Jew, and I am a Samaritan — so how can you ask me for a drink?" (Jews will not drink from the same cups and bowls that Samaritans use.)

John 4:7-9
New American Bible

- What are the Scriptures saying to us regarding prejudice?

- Why has Jesus' example at the well been so difficult for us to follow?

Social Inquiry

The 1960s and '70s were decades of turmoil and change. As we gaze back through those times from the vantage point of the mid-80s, we see how much we have accomplished, how far we have come.

Blacks are no longer forced to use separate facilities or sit in the back of the bus.

Females no longer must marry to have a place in society. Education and job opportunities in any field are open to women.

Little girls don't have to be cheerleaders, but can play on the teams alongside the little boys.

Handicapped access to buildings and facilities such as restrooms, telephones, and curbstones, welcomes handicapped citizens into the public eye. "Public Law 94-142 attempts to assure the rights of the handicapped. Their parents and guardians are protected by tying the adequacy of local services to federal subsidies underwriting the costs of special education programs for the handicapped."

Older Americans have been liberated from their rocking chairs. Medicare and Social Security help to insure their quality of life.

Males are encouraged to cry, to express their feelings and to enjoy the nurturing of relationships.

Our task in this meeting is to re-examine these issues. No discussion on families making peace would be complete without a re-evaluation of our growth and progress along the lines of combating Ageism, Racism, Sexism, and Chauvinism and our personal attitudes toward them.

Special Children An Integrative Approach
Bernard G. Shaw/Joseph V. Rizzo
Scott Foresman & Co., 1983

From Your Own Personal Experience, **OBSERVE**:

1. Before the next meeting, be on the lookout for and make note of 3 incidents of injustice toward minorities (racial or ethnic groups, women, the elderly, the disabled.)

2. What were or are your parents' attitudes toward these people? Recount three incidents that illustrate the effect of their attitudes on their grandchildren.

3. Ask three people for their opinion on how much progress has been made on these issues.

A good leader is one who makes it possible for everyone to contribute to the group.

In Light of Christ's Teachings, JUDGE:

1. What effect has holding differing attitudes had on your relationship with the people closest to you? How has this affected the peace between you and those closest to you? (family, neighbors, co-workers, etc.)
2. How can we balance our concern for Justice and the acceptance of the attitudes of those for whom we care?
3. What responsibility do we have to correct injustice where we find it? (For example, when a check-out clerk is rude to an elderly customer, should we intervene-shatter the peace-by coming to the elderly person's defense?)
4. What is the root of injustice, if injustice is the root of lack of peace?
5. What moral obligation does a Christian have to work for justice?
6. What is our responsibility to make our views known to those who hold stereotyped views on these (above-mentioned) people?

From What Has Been Discussed, Decide How You Can **ACT:**

1. Within your church take some steps to remedy the plight of one of the groups of people herein mentioned.
a) Do you have wheelchair ramps?
b) Do women play a significant role in the life of the parish?
c) Does the wisdom and experience of senior citizens get put to use or is it wasted?
2. Read the book, *In A Different Voice*, by Carol Gilligan, Harvard University Press.
3. Invite a representative of a Thomas Merton Center, Parenting for Peace and Justice, Pax Christi, or other peace and justice organization, to a future meeting to present their purpose and methods for promoting peace and justice.
4. Think twice before laughing at or repeating jokes which are derogatory to any group of people.

Before deciding on an **Act**, read and reflect on the

following:

> No society can live in peace with itself, or with the world, without a full awareness of the worth and dignity of every human person, and of the sacredness of all human life (Jas 4:1-2). When we accept violence, war itself can be taken for granted. Violence has many faces: oppression of the poor, deprivation of basic human rights, economic exploitation, sexual exploitation and pornography, neglect or abuse of the aged and helpless, and innumerable other acts of inhumanity.
> The Challenge of Peace: God's Promise and Our Response
> A Pastoral Letter on War and Peace

Write the Act you intend to do and share it with the group.

Look ahead to the Observes for the next meeting.

Peace Trivia   Did you know who said . . .
"Every rocket that is fired, every warship that is launched in the final sense is a theft from those who are hungry."
Dwight D. Eisenhower

Reactions to *Peaceworks* were both positive and negative. As in earlier programs the Inquiries posed challenges to CFMers to see the world with new eyes. Peter and Mary Sawada from Tokyo, Japan, reported: "We are just using the Japanese translation of *Peaceworks*. We just finished the fourth inquiry. We invited a Catholic news reporter to our October meeting to learn about CFM and get acquainted with our program. We have found a person who has agreed to brush up the Japanese in our translation of *Peaceworks*.

From another perspective, Pat Foley, one of the editors, wrote:

> We've been in CFM nine years and I never remember a year full of comments on the program like *Peaceworks* generated. Some positive and encouraging, others reporting hurt feelings and anger. People were threatening to quit CFM.

She reflects on how the negative letters affected their family:

> Even one of our teenagers was affected. After reading a particularly disheartening series of letters to the editor (in *ACT*), Gaele sat down and wrote a letter in reply to those critics. The gist of it was, how dare those Rambo-ists talk to my parents like that! I cautioned her against mailing it though because she had allowed her adolescent anger to be vented — and as anyone who lives with a teenager knows — adolescent anger is a great shatterer of peace. I had written a reply myself to the letters and when Gaele read my response, she claimed I was "wimping out" — explaining and apologizing for the book. "If I can't send mine 'cause it's too strong, you certainly can't send yours 'cause it's too weak!" she declared. We compromised and sent neither.
>
> In light of the events like Challenger and Chernobyl — *Peaceworks* was right. We witnessed the tragedies and I was reminded of not placing my faith in "Gods of Metal," not to worship technology as the ultimate answer.
>
> I hope everyone can at least agree with the front cover of *Peaceworks* and along with St. Matthew hope "with God all things are possible" and continue to work to bring about peace.

The program, *Peacemaking*, was based on the U.S. Bishops' Peace Pastoral. In 1987, the implementation of the the Pastoral Letter on the Economy was the focus of the Christian Family Movement. Titled, *Family Values in the Marketplace: Spending Our Time, Spending Our Money*, the program asks families to confront the hard issues facing the people of America.

The Inquiries in *Family Values in the Marketplace* deal with Life on the Farm; Unemployment; Strangers in Our Midst; Sanctuary; Immigration; the Feminization of Poverty; Family Finances and Changing Times; At Home with the Kids; Does the Church Practice the Justice which It Preaches? Where Is the Church in All This? Simple Life Styles; Unions. Each meeting is concerned with one of the sections of the Pastoral Letter.

Using the wisdom of the lived experience of families, the Inquiries are written by farm families in the Midwest, members of the Sanctuary Movement in California, citizens in Miami, Florida, and a third-generation union member in Michigan. Other couples in Colorado, Illinois, and Pennsylvania write on topics which immediately impinge on family life. For example, consumerism.

The CFM Convention at St. Mary's College in South Bend focuses on the Pastoral Letter on the Economy. Besides celebrating together as families, renewing friendships and making new ones, adults concentrate on various workshops. Some offerings: Confessions of a Christian Capitalist, It's Good Business; The Heart of Family Life: Compassion and Prayer; The Genius of Habitat for Humanity; Hunger, Its Causes and Our Response; Exploring the Economics Pastoral: Tension with the Mainstream Culture; Sponsoring Refugees; Children and Money, a Progressive Guide.

Not to be outdone, teenagers share their own special program. On this family convention-vacation, no one is left out. Skilled babysitters for the under-three and creative activities for the four-to-elevens fall in the competent hands of student teachers from St. Mary's College.

Family Values in the Marketplace, the CFM program for 1987, continues the long history CFM began in the '50s to educate and activate families in the work of peace and justice. Focusing on the Gospel, Encyclicals, and other church documents, the people in the pews are invited to Observe-Judge-Act, to confront the Gospel question, "What is asked of me?", and to emphasize practical and realizable actions.

The challenges to CFMers are not new, nor will they disappear. Don and Barbara Thorman were pioneers in CFM. In the April, 1960 issue of *ACT*, Don wrote:

> CFM has been in the business well over a decade now. What is the purpose of the Movement? Is it to reconstruct

society, economics, politics, family life, religion, recreation, education? If so, we have not accomplished much.

Is it to Christianize family life alone? Does any CFMer claim that the climate of family life has changed significantly during the past ten years among Catholic families or in the broader American community? If our purpose is to change society or its institutions and make them "Christian," can CFM or any other Catholic group accomplish such a purpose? We think not.

America is not a Catholic nation. It is made up of Catholics, Jews, Protestants, non-believers and other groups. This means two problems are involved. One is the education and formation of well-trained and practicing Catholics. It is no secret that all Catholics are not well-educated in the social teachings of the Church. The other problem is that of making an impact on the larger community.

The problems are vitally concerned with our community, national, even international. Ultimately, CFM's impact will be made through its members who will act as responsible citizens in the affairs of the community.

Seventeen years later, before his untimely death in 1977, Don spoke editorially in the *National Catholic Reporter* from another perspective. He said:

Today those of us who still believe in the institution, its ultimate values and our spiritual heritage must learn to make do. We don't have enough time left in our lives to wait for the theologians and the official magisterial forces to work out a modus vivendi. The *now* we live in demands that we live as best we can, making our own decisions based on the best information available to us and formation of our consciences.

Our sacrifice for the future of the institution and its unborn members is to live patiently and with fortitude while a very necessary struggle between honest freedom and deadening monarchical-hierarchical force from the past works itself out. We shall survive because we know the real life of the church is in the faith-community.

Frankly, today I'm worried and wary. I'm worried about

my church which is in disarray. And I'm wary of all the theologians, liberal and conservative .... I have learned there is only one person I can entrust with my faith and my soul — me. While all the discussion, debates and deliberations go on, my decision-making cannot come to a standstill. Many of the issues might not be resolved until long after I'm dead. In the meantime, I'm still responsible for myself and, frankly, I cannot think of any human being I'd be willing to follow indiscriminately.

The institutional church and the theologians all have something to tell me and to teach me. I'll listen, even respectfully. But recent experience has taught me more than ever before that I must think, speak, and act for myself. Somehow I don't think I'll be given the opportunity at the judgment seat to turn my defense over to a theologian or institutional official.

Don Thorman, who gave his great heart and talent to the service of the church, was the epitome of men and women today. The call Don made was to himself and others to be faithful to the Gospel message, as far as humanly possible in a fragmented world.

We learned from Monsignor Hillenbrand, "Ignorance of Scripture is ignorance of Christ, the Way, the Truth and the Life, and deprives members of a tool for their own spiritual progress and for action in the parish. Action does *not* precede development. They take place simultaneously. Development through action is essential. Action is a love of Christ through love of others. A mere intellectual development is sterile unless it is used to love others ... by direct action or by refashioning institutions which mold human life."

Life can never be the same for all who walk the challenging journey in CFM.

"And who is my neighbor?" The question has been asked in every generation as people attempt to live their lives responding to the call of Jesus. For forty years couples and families of the Christian Family Movement have struggled with the same question in a world remarkably different from the world of Jesus' time and, yet, a world remarkably the same.

Our world of differing beliefs is fragmented by classes, ages, lifestyles, customs. We are the first people to see our earth-home from outer space, to realize that we are inextricably tied to the marvellous planet God designed for us. Our world is still circumscribed by our limited knowledge; Jesus' world was the same.

Our world is beset by the terrible problems of hunger, sexism, torture, discrimination, hatred and lack of love between peoples. Jesus' world was the same. In both worlds the question, "And who is my neighbor?" has caused people to tremble and turn away.

The Christian Family Movement is not a panacea for all the ills of our age. It is a place for people to gather together to struggle with and to try to bring to life the Gospel of Christ in a new time and a new place.

This continuing story of the visionaries and adventurers of the late 1940s, who came together to form the Christian Family Movement, is the story of thousands of families of the world — people on a journey, wanting to heal some of the wounds of their age, however imperfect their actions. The map of the journey to live the Gospel of our time is still sketchy and sometimes hidden. It is a map with limited marking, a map through uncharted territory. The journey remains uniquely ours as people baptized in the priesthood of Jesus Christ.

Prayer of the Christian Family Movement
Almighty and eternal God, may your Grace enkindle
in all love for the many unfortunate people whom
poverty and misery reduce to a condition of life
unworthy of human beings.
Arouse in the hearts of those who call you Father,
a hunger and thirst for social justice and for
charity in deeds and in truth. Grant, O Lord, peace
in our days, peace to souls, peace to families, peace

to our country, peace among nations.

Holy Year prayer of Pius XII
Prayer of the Christian Family Movement

PROGRAMS OF THE CHRISTIAN FAMILY MOVEMENT
1951-1987

1951 — Social Pressures Affecting Parent-Child Relationships
1952 — Civic Responsibility, Work, and Recreation
1952 — For Happier Families
1953 — Social Responsibility, Family Finances, Education
1954 — Community in Parish, School, Society
1955 — The Layman's Role in the Church
1956 — Social Harmony
1957 — For Happier Families — Fifth Edition
1957 — Parish Life and Education
1958 — A Guide to CFM
1958 — Family Life and Economics
1959 — Politics and Christian Life
1960 — International Life
1961 — The Family, Center of Social Rebirth
1962 — Christianity and Social Progress
1963 — The Parish, Leaven of the Community
1964 — Encounter in Politics and Race
1965 — The Creator Has Made the World, Come and See It
1966 — The Family in a Time of Change
1967 — Building Community
1968 — Shalom-Peace
1969 — People Are...
1970 — The Family in Time of Revolution
1971 — The Quality of Life
1972 — Love Happens
1972 — Institutions and the Family
1973 — Discovering Christ
1973 — The Encountering Family

1973 — The Encountering Couple
1974 — Love Happens in Families
1975 — Discovering Me
1975 — Ministering Together (chaplains)
1975 — Discovering Others
1975 — Why World Hunger
1975 — FIND — Families Involved in Nurture and Development
1976 — Work, Money and Your Family
1977 — Understanding and Building Community
1978 — Parent Enrichment Manual
1978 — And Then Came the Dawn of a New Day — Death and Dying
1978 — Revaluing the Christian Commitment
1978 — Introduction to CFM
1979 — Your Marriage the Great Adventure
1979 — Come Through Life With Me
1979 — Leading in the Christian Style
1979 — Building Happiness Thru Christ — I
1980 — Your Family Called to Action
1980 — The Dawn of a New Day, revised
1980 — Building Happiness Thru Christ — II
1981 — In Search of Jesus (teen book)
1981 — Quality of Life Renewed
1982 — The Eve of Orwell
1982 — People Are..., revised
1983 — Hope and Promise (divorce)
1984 — People of Faith
1985 — Peaceworks
1986 — Becoming Family
1987 — Family Values in the Marketplace, Justice for All

INDEX

Adam, Karl, xi
Ahman, Matt, 58
Aitchison, Kay and Gary, v, xiii, 12, 102, 110
Alcocer, Antonio and Christina, 98
Aldrich, Bob and Janet, 94, 95, 96
Alvarez-Icaza, Pepe and Luzma, 50, 58
Ambrose, Michael, 65
Andrews, Jim, 76, 78
Aviano, Nelly de, 58
Arns, Paolo Evaristo, 109
Baldwin, Pat, 45
Banneker, Benjamin, 77
Barlow, Vince, 109
Barnor, Edi and Magdalena, 98
Bauchat, Shari and Bob, 92
Bauer, Helen and Bernie, iv, 10, 40, 46
Baum, Gregory, 58,
Berrigan, Dan, 58
Berryman, Phillip, 68
Bonsignore, Madelyn and Joe, v, 58, 86
Bosc, Robert, 43
Burgraff, Cathy and Bob, 12
Buswell, Charles, iv, 58, 83, 84
Caldwell, Laura and Bill, xiii, 5, 21, 23, 63
Callahan, Sydney, 34
Calvo, Gabriel, 47, 48
Camara, Helder, 50
Cantwell, Ed, 90
Cardijn, Joseph, iv, ix, x, 10, 26
Carlo, Barbara and Armando, 89
Carola, Estelle and Mario, 35, 113
Carr, Betsy and Jim, 68
Carr, Jim and Betsy, 68
Caulfield, Genevieve, 57
Cipar, Dan, 84
Clark, Bill, 83
Cody, John, 71
Coffield, John, xi
Congar, Yves, xi
Crowley, Pat and Patty, iv, xi, xiii, 11, 12, 23, 29, 30, 40, 42, 50, 58, 69, 71, 88
Cummings Family, 45
Curnow, John, 58
Curran, Dolores, xi
Dale, Vernie and Tom, 25, 109
Daly, Bernard, 51
Daly, John and Helen, 67
Davilla, Rafael and Berta, 49
Davis, Klarise, iv
Dearden, John, 88
Donnelly, Dody, 32
Dooley, Tom, 58
Drish, Dorothy and John, xiii, 38, 39
Dyson, Bill, 55
Eckert, Bill, 92
Edgerly, Leo and Myrtle, 16, 17
Egan, John, 67
Eitel, John and Pat, 69
Ellis, John Tracy, 58

Ensroth, Ray and Eleanor
Erviti, Gustavo Isabel, 49
Eschweiler, Ed and Fran, iv
Fernandez, Angelo, 80
Ferrara, Sal and Stephanie, 67
Fichter, Joseph, 18, 34, 61
Fischer, Earl, 51
Fisher, Charles and Kerry, 25
Fitton, Edward F., 92
Fitzgerald, Maureen, 57
Fitzpatrick, Dan and Donna, 58
Flores, Patricio, 49
Foley, Pat, 96, 112, 114
Foley, Gaele, 123
Fonder, Al and Jane, 54
Ford, Josephine, 58
Fox, Bob, 90
Friere, Paolo, 52, 53
Froehlich, Edwina, 47
Furlong, Bill and Barbara, 46
Gacnik, Pat and Frank, 93, 94, 111
Garcia, John, 16, 17, 36, 83, 84
Geaney, Dennis, v, 16, 18, 83, 86, 87
Getlein, Frank, 57
Gillespie, Jerry, 25
Gleason, Peg and Ed, 84
Glickman, Dan, 78
Gorciak, George and Gen, 46
Greeley, Andrew, 67
Greene, Michael, 51
Gremillion, Joseph, 51
Guardini, Romano, xi
Guppenberger, August, 46
Hallem, Ed, 83
Hamilton, Sue and Wayne, 54, 109, 110
Hammel, Ed, 86
Haring, Bernard, 18, 34
Harland, Marge and Dan, xii
Hartke, Vance, 76
Hassett, Jim and Helen, 67
Hatfield, Mark, 76, 78

Hayes, John, 44
Healey, Kathleen, 84
Hellegers, Andre, 71
Hesburgh, Theodore, 55, 76, 78
Hillenbrand, Reynold, 14, 15, 21, 26, 31, 32, 40, 58, 63, 71, 75, 125
Hochbrueckner, George and Carol Ann, 106, 107
Hogan, Ed, 83
Hollinde, Betty, 46
Houtart, Francois, 57
Hug, James E., 11, 52
Hurley, Frank, 83
John XXIII, ix, xi, xiii, 52, 72, 74, 75, 101, 102
Johnson, Ernest and Elizabeth, 36
Johnson, Lyndon, 76
Jones, Arthur, iv
Jones, Margaret and Don, 40
Joyce, Brian, 83
Judge, John and Florence, 18, 19
Kanaly, Don, 83
Kelly, Larry, 67
Kennedy, Tom, 51
Kohler, Ed, 83, 87
Kohler, Mary Conway, 97
Landregan, Steve and Virginia, 50, 51
Lennon, Viola, 47
Leroux, Roly and Isabelle, 54
Lichten, Joseph, 58
Ligutti, Luisgi, 57
Lovett, Vincent, 51
Lucey, Dan and Rose, v, 40, 72, 75, 78, 79
Lundquist, Chuck and Stella, 21
Mabley, Jack, 42
MacKenzie, John L., 34, 80
MacMahon, Bob and Kate, xii
Mallon, John, 108
Manning, Timothy, 68
Marin, Francis, 36
Maritain, Jacques and Raissa, xi

Maldoon, Dorothy and Ray, 12, 29, 38, 88
Marty, Martin, 58
Massura, Mary and Joe, 45
Matsunaga, Spark, 78
McAllister, Elizabeth, 80
McCarthy, John, 108
McCarthy, Eugene, 34
McClellan, Don, 54
McCoy, Bill and Gladys, 37
McIntyre, James Francis, 67, 68
McMahon, Bill, 83
McNulty, Bill, 83
Mead, Margaret, 97, 98, 99
Metzler, Warren, 113
Meyer, Albert, 52
Mignon, Odette and Jacques, 43
Mili, Jude, 45, 111
Miller, Kathleen, 47
Mimiaga, Lena and Bill, iv
Monroe, Marilyn, 32
Montcheuil, Yves de, xi
Montgomery, James W., 27
Moran, Charles, 65
Moreira, Lucas, 50
Moriarty, Pat and Joe, 19
Mulhern, Ray, 45
Munier, Joseph, 35, 83
Murnane, Tim, 51
Murphy, Raymond, 83
Murray, John Courtney, xi
Nathe, Paul and Irene, 46
Nelson, Marianne, 51
Nerin, Bill, 83
Noonan, John, 57, 69, 81
Nouwen, Henri, 58, 80, 81
Nyerere, Julius, 42
Nyirenda, Sara, 53
O'Brien, Leo, 89
O'Connell, Dan and Mary, 51, 69
O'Neill, Bill, 86
O'Rourke Family, 46
Page, Annie, 90
Pattin, Pat and Kathy, 37

Paul VI, 69, 71
Pavan, Pietro, 58
Payne, Joseph, 83, 85
Peters, Bill, 83, 110
Piantadosi, Arthur and Cecil, xii
Pius XII, 128
Poux, John, 69
Printz, Dan and Judy, 102
Prus, Elizabeth, xii
Putz, Louis, iv, 10, 32, 40, 56, 57, 87
Quigley, Martin and Katherine, 57
Rachel, Bernie, 86
Ramirez, Pat and Lupe, 35
Randall, Don and Joan, 62
Reedy, John, 76, 78
Reid, Elizabeth, 57
Richards, Pedro, 49
Ricks, Tom, 108
Rivers, Clarence, 59
Rummel, Joseph Francis, 34
Rush, Benjamin, 77
Ryan, Barba and Jerry, 52
Ryan, Mary Perkins, 57
Sammon, Peter, iv
Saunders, Joe and Lee, 91
Scalise, Charlie and Cathy, 68, 69
Schuster, George, 58
Sheed, Frank, 13
Shriver, Sargent, 68
Simon, Paul, 58
Sison, Sito and Sony, 111
Sittler, Joseph, 58
Smith, Paul, 113
Smith, Kathleen, 113
Sober, Bob and Laverne, 109
Sonneville, Tina, 110
Springer, Betty and Herb, xiii
Stokes, Carl, 34
Strenski Family, 45
Suenens, Leon Joseph, 15, 116
Suhard, Emanuel, 15
Sullivan, Jack and Audrey, 23, 24
Sylvain, Barbara, 51

Syrianey, Ted, 58, 83
Taiso, Bessie and Eddie, 49
Taylor, Ned and Louise, 44
Teilhard de Chardin, 41, 59
Theresa of Calcutta, 80
Thomas, John L., 18, 55
Thorman, Don and Barbara, 51, 124, 125
Tomanto, Bob and Irene, 54, 89, 90
Tompson, Marian, 47
Toohey, Jim, 69
Twomey, Louis, 58
Uttich Family, 45
Valdes, Alecia, 111
Valenti, Paul, 58, 83

Van Belleghem, Dan, 108
Yogel, Bill and Mary Kay, 90, 107
Wagner, Jim, 69
Wagner, Betty, 47
Walthers, Miriam, 113
Weber, Gerald, 85
Weigel, Gustav, 58
Weissert, Ralph and Reggie, iv, xiii, 40, 56, 76, 91
Weisshaar, Marlene, iv
White, Mary, 47
Witt, Vern and Maureen, 62
Wohler Family, 45
Wolgamot, Ted, Pete, Marguerite, 111
Wynns, Jack and Dorothy, xii

For information on CFM, write:
Christian Family Movement
PO Box 272
Ames, IA 50010

To write to the author:
Rose Marciano Lucey
750 Oakland Ave., Apt. 106
Oakland, CA 94611